Napoleon Bonaparte, the Corsican who became Napoleon I, Emperor of the French, has compelled the world's imagination more strongly perhaps than any other man in history. He has been looked upon as everything from a new Messiah to the devil himself, even the Beast of the Apocalypse; and there has grown up around his name a mass of stories and myths which have clouded the true story of the 'Little Corporal'. But, as Albert Guérard shows in this masterly new study, the real Napoleon is quite as remarkable and fascinating a figure as the legendary one. He claimed that he was not ambitious; but he had an unquenchable thirst for glory, and honours, wealth, even power itself, were but means to satisfy that relentless desire. To Napoleon, the 'morrow of every victory is an anti-climax: there m

prodigies, each

NAPOLEON I

THE STRATFORD LIBRARY

NAPOLEON I

ALBERT GUÉRARD

HUTCHINSON OF LONDON

HUTCHINSON & CO. (*Publishers*) LTD
178–202 Great Portland Street, London, W.1

London Melbourne Sydney
Auckland Bombay Toronto
Johannesburg New York

★

First published 1957

*Set in ten point Caledonia one point leaded
and printed in Great Britain by
Taylor Garnett Evans & Co. Ltd
Watford, Hertfordshire*

FOR

my granddaughters

Mary Maclin and Lucy Lundie Guérard

To read when they are seven

CONTENTS

Foreword   11

1 Young Buonaparte, 1769—1795   17

2 General Bonaparte; *Rehearsals for Empire:
   Italy and Egypt*, 1796—1799   33

3 The Man of the Hour; *Bonaparte First Consul*,
   1799—1802   48

4 The Parting of the Ways; *Napoleon Bonaparte*:
   Consul for Life, 1802—1804   65

5 Napoleon Emperor; *The Ascending Star*,
   1804—1807   82

6 Dark Omens, 1808—1809   100

7 Splendours and Miseries, 1810—1811   121

8 Downfall; *The Russian Campaign*, 1812   134

9 The German and the French Campaigns,
   1813—1814   155

10 Elba and the Hundred Days, 1814—1815   170

11 Epilogue; *St. Helena*, 1815—1821. Paris, 1840   191

   Note on Sources   202

   Index   209

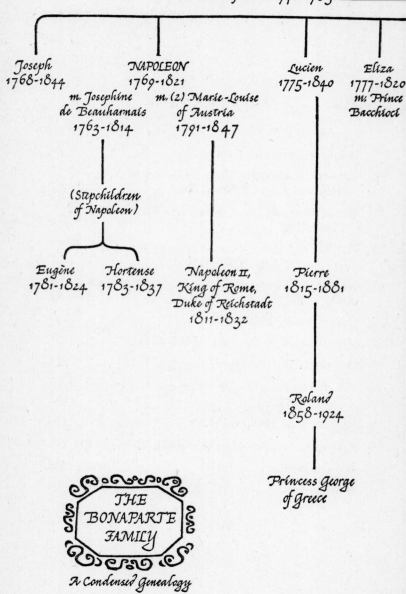

Carlo Buonaparte (1746-1785)

Joseph
1768-1844
m. Josephine
de Beauharnais
1763-1814

NAPOLEON
1769-1821
m. (2) Marie-Louise
of Austria
1791-1847

Lucien
1775-1840

Eliza
1777-1820
m. Prince
Bacchioci

(Stepchildren
of Napoleon)

Eugène
1781-1824

Hortense
1783-1837

Napoleon II,
King of Rome,
Duke of Reichstadt
1811-1832

Pierre
1815-1881

Roland
1858-1924

Princess George
of Greece

THE
BONAPARTE
FAMILY

A Condensed Genealogy

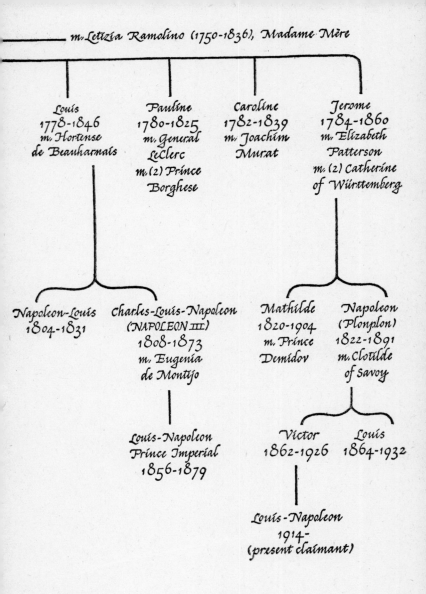

m. Letizia Ramolino (1750-1836), Madame Mère

Louis
1778-1846
m. Hortense
de Beauharnais

Pauline
1780-1825
m. General
LeClerc
m. (2) Prince
Borghese

Caroline
1782-1839
m. Joachim
Murat

Jerome
1784-1860
m. Elizabeth
Patterson
m. (2) Catherine
of Württemberg

Napoleon-Louis
1804-1831

Charles-Louis-Napoleon
(NAPOLEON III)
1808-1873
m. Eugenia
de Montijo

Mathilde
1820-1904
m. Prince
Demidov

Napoleon
(Plonplon)
1822-1891
m. Clotilde
of Savoy

Louis-Napoleon
Prince Imperial
1856-1879

Victor
1862-1926

Louis
1864-1932

Louis-Napoleon
1914-
(present claimant)

BIOGRAPHY, HISTORY, LEGEND

THIS will be the story of a *human* life. Of the multitudinous writings about Napoleon—over one hundred thousand, according to Kircheisen—many place him beyond our common humanity. For Victor Hugo, Léon Bloy, Dmitri Merezhkovsky, and Dr. McNair Wilson, he was *L'Homme, The Man*, in a messianic sense. In his lifetime, pious souls in England considered him as a fiend spewed from hell; and Pierre Bezúkhov, the hero of Tolstoys *War and Peace*, spent laborious hours seeking to establish that his number was that of the Beast, six hundred and sixty-six. Even Taine, who posed as a realist and a positivist, tried to make our flesh creep with suggestions that Napoleon, under the semblance of a man, belonged to another race and another time: an aerolith from outer space, or, in Mallarmé's words, "a block fallen here below from some obscure disaster". For others, he was not a historical character at all, but undiluted myth, as he himself believed of Jesus Christ; J. B. Pérès and Archbishop Whately devoted clever little books to the proposition that Napoleon never existed.

After fifty years of study, Napoleon appears to me as neither angel nor beast, but as human, all too human: our brother—our Big Brother—a creature of strong but ailing flesh, lean and sulphurous in youth, paunchy and lardy in middle life; not a very good husband, who married two not very good wives; a martinet, an incomparable efficiency manager, with an addiction to gambling and gigantic dreams.

Napoleon belongs to history: it is through his career that we know his personality. He made history; but first history made him. What would the tense Corsican boy have been, with the same passions and the same devouring energy, if he had been born a few decades earlier or later? Another Rousseau perhaps—that Rousseau with whom he once compared himself? Or a Balzac? Balzac had on his desk a statuette of the Emperor with the defiant words: "What he failed to accomplish with the sword, I shall achieve with the pen"[1] Who can tell? As indications, we have two admirable studies of the Napoleonic temper under totally different circumstances: Julian Sorel, the hero of Stendhal's *The Red and the Black*, and Rastignac, who in Balzac's *Father Goriot* challenges Paris to mortal combat. Archives provide only the incidents and the trappings, those things which were common to Bonaparte and Augereau or Masséna; the drama of Napoleon is in Napoleon's soul. And to that inner drama Stendhal and Balzac offer a better clue than Thiers or Madelin. For Napoleon is a hero of romance who happened to traverse history.

The relations between biography and history remain a baffling problem. Carlyle believed in "heroes", Emerson in "representative men", Napoleon III in "Providential men", Hitler in the Leader by right of divine election. On the other hand, Tolstoy, with painful elaboration, expounds his doctrine that there are no leaders at all. The strutting little figures are swept away by the flood they pathetically commanded to rise or to recede. Napoleon gave wrong orders, which were not obeyed; had they been obeyed, it would have made no difference.

[1] i.e., to create a world. Napoleon looms enormously larger than Balzac; but the Balzacian world is more alive than the Napoleonic.

The greatness of Kutusov was that he gave no orders at all. A wilful paradox? It sounds less absurd in connection with the Russian campaign than with any other great event in history. It does not make sense: it denies sense. But the hypothesis that Napoleon, a political and military genius of unequalled magnitude, was, intellectually and morally, in full control of the forces that carried him to Moscow, is an even more flagrant absurdity. We must remember also that reputable historians—Adolphe Thiers, Albert Sorrel, Jacques Bainville—maintain that the course of Napoleon, ascent and decline, was determined by the conquest of the Rhine frontier in 1795: it would have been futile for the heir of the Revolution to decree that "the Trojan War could not take place".[1] Napoleon himself had a strange deep-seated belief in "Destiny", a power beyond human computation and human will. This would not affect the appeal of his tragedy: Oedipus also was the plaything of relentless fate.

On a less mystic plane, it may be asserted that history is made up of immense processes. Science can describe and explain them, for they are subject to laws; but in their majestic sweep, the share of any individual is infinitesimal. The Reformation is greater than Luther or Calvin; the Enlightenment absorbs Voltaire and Diderot; James Watt stands only for an incident in the Industrial Revolution. Great men are not causes, but names used as symbols for great events: just as Waterloo is merely a village where the famous battle was *not* fought. History is not a string of anecdotes. Again, Napoleon saw deeper than some of his worshippers: he was conscious of that obscure power which he called *la force des choses*, the irresistible might of things. On the proper scale, it would be possible to record the advances and regressions

1 Jean Giraudoux: *La Guerre de Troie n'aura pas lieu,* written on the eve of World War II.

of the nineteenth century without mentioning Napoleon at all. If this be the case, then let us admit that the present book is not written on the proper scale.

Finally, it may be contended that, as history is the collective memory of mankind, events and men are "historical" in so far as they are "memorable". Not because they are great: Mme Dubarry is better remembered than Condillac. Not even because they are true: most famous sayings on record are apocryphal. But because they are impressive, for the memory of the race is swayed by dreads and hopes. This factor, sentimental and aesthetic rather than scientific, constitutes the *Legend*. The legend may have a nucleus of solid fact: there actually was a Charlemagne, though the hero of the epic cycle, nearly three centuries later, was a different personage. There may have been a King Arthur, though Tennyson did his best to make him incredible. There probably never was a William Tell—the only Swiss who lives in the hearts of men. Was there an early prototype of Prometheus?

In the case of Napoleon, the Legend is enormously more significant than sober history. Every study of the Napoleonic theme should begin with a thorough investigation of the Legend. Let this be done with no thought of "debunking", a process as vulgar as its name; but in order to disengage the plain palpable truth from the folk epic, the modern *Iliad* or *Nibelungenlied*. Because they have neglected this initial step, many painstaking scholars like Frédéric Masson, Louis Madelin, and Kircheisen have simply studded the Legend—unchallenged—with innumerable realistic facts. With the same method they could have written a learned monograph on Nicholas, Bishop of Myra, and retain untarnished their childlike faith in Santa Claus. Perhaps they would not have worked so diligently if they had not been sustained by that faith.

I have attempted elsewhere,[1] not to offer a survey of that illimitable field, but to indicate a path of approach. In the present book, which is pure biography, I propose to ignore the Legend almost entirely. The result may at times appear disconcerting. What! A Napoleon without the "whiff of grapeshot", a Napoleon who lost six campaigns out of twelve, a Napoleon who botched the Concordat and allowed himself to be hoodwinked by Talleyrand and Fouché! I cannot, however, leave the Legend out of account altogether, because Napoleon was, deliberately and with magnificent success, the poet of his own saga. The "glory" for which he craved and to which he erected altars was an aura transforming drab reality. That is why St. Helena, where with marvellous skill he reinterpreted his personage, remains the most successful of his campaigns. It was not for immediate power that he was playing his part, but in order to impress posterity. He had his wish: his empire is dust, but his fame has lost none of its splendour. A life of Napoleon that would exclude Napoleon the Artist—*commediante! tragediante!* —would be *Hamlet* without the Prince.

ALBERT GUÉRARD.

[1] *Reflections on the Napoleonic Legend* (London and New York, 1924).

CHAPTER ONE

YOUNG BUONAPARTE

1769—1795

O N Assumption Day, 15 August, 1769, Mme Letizia Buonaparte was attending Mass at Ajaccio when she felt the first pangs of childbirth. She hurried home, had no time to reach her bedroom, and, on a sofa downstairs, was delivered of a son. No doctor was there to assist her, not even a midwife. She was nineteen, and in the five years of her married life she had already borne three children; only one, Joseph, survived. Little Napoleone —in the Corsican dialect Nabulione—was puny but well formed. He was entering life at a critical moment in the history of his country.

Corsica, which travel posters proclaim "the isle of Beauty": a tight little world, stern and wild like Caledonia, but under happier skies; harsh, mountainous, forest-clad; the flat eastern shore marshy and fever-ridden; the habitable valleys fertile enough, but isolated by abrupt ranges into distinct communities, especially in those days when highways were little better than mule trails. The untilled slopes were thickly covered with shrubs—arbutus, myrtle, thorn, laurel, and broom—the tang of which reached even to the sea. This wasteland was the *maquis* (*macchia*): a name which, through Émile Zola in 1898 and the *Résistance* in World War II, has became known through the world. After a *vendetta* or

blood feud the outlaws would seek sanctuary in that
aromatic wilderness. Gentlemen avenging their honour
were at times hard to distinguish from cut-throats;
banditry remained endemic in the highlands of Corsica
until the very end of the nineteenth century. A little over
three thousand square miles of ruggedness, poverty, and
pride. Only fifty miles away lay the coast of Tuscany,
then under the rule of Leopold, mild and liberal like his
brother the Emperor Joseph II; a hundred miles to the
north was Genoa, in resplendent decrepitude; a little
farther, the France of the Enlightenment. The miles
might have been centuries.

Aloof Corsica was invaded by all the peoples who
ever sailed the Mediterranean: Ligurians and Etruscans
in dim antiquity, Phoenicians from Carthage, Greeks
from Phocæa, Romans, Vandals, Goths, Lombards,
Byzantines, Saracens. It remained untamed, like its larger
neighbour Sardinia, while Sicily was repeatedly a
splendid centre of culture. In the Middle Ages possession
of the island was in dispute between Pisa and Genoa: the
aristocracy of Corsica came from those two cities. At the
end of the thirteenth century Genoa, farther away but
stronger at sea, remained in uneasy control. The open
fight for Corsican independence filled the whole of the
eighteenth century. A Westphalian adventurer, Baron
Theodor von Neuhof, made himself king and achieved
immortality by figuring, with other deposed monarchs,
in a chapter of Voltaire's *Candide*. The island might have
been left to its fragrant primitiveness and to its medieval
chaos—a loose confederacy of small cities or *communes*—
but for the complex rivalries of Genoa, Sardinia, France,
and Great Britain. The islanders did manage at last to
achieve a rough unity under Pasquale Paoli (1725-1807),
whose father and brother had already led them against
the Genoese. With superb assurance the Corsicans

created a "university" in the village of Corte, their inland
capital, and requested Jean-Jacques Rousseau to draft
their constitution. The Republic of Genoa, long past its
prime, could not cope with the rebellion and called upon
the French for assistance. For decades there was a fitful,
ambiguous condominium. Finally, despairing of subduing
the wild unprofitable country, the Genoese sold the
shadow of their rights to Louis XV (15 May, 1768).

In such a primitive country the few civilized families
stood out, though by Continental standards their posses-
sions and their learning might have seemed scanty. Carlo
Buonaparte (1746-85), Napoleon's father, attended a
Jesuit school at Ajaccio and pursued his law studies at
the "university" of Corte; but his wife, Letizia, *née*
Ramolino, though of good stock, never felt at home in
Italian or French; even after she had become the mother
of many kings, she gladly relapsed into her native patois.
Young Carlo was an ardent supporter of Paoli. He took
part in the last victory of free Corsica, at Borgo, and
perhaps in the final defeat at Ponte Nuovo (8 March,
1769). It was said that the intrepid Letizia was with him,
and the unborn Napoleon. The Paolists were over-
whelmed; the leader and some three hundred and fifty
of his followers, rescued by two British ships, sought
refuge in England.

The battle was lost; but for Carlo, only twenty-three
years of age, there was ample time to win another. He
refused to entangle his young destiny with a losing cause,
and whole-heartedly joined the French party. History
finds it difficult to pass judgement on "collaborationists".
The name is attached, opprobriously, to Laval and
Quisling; but it would fit also Marshal Smuts and
Emperor Hirohito. At any rate, Carlo showed no lack of
decision. He went to take his law degree at Pisa so as to
qualify himself for action on a larger scale; and,

characteristically, he spent a year's income in celebrating the event. Vanity and shrewdness were combined in him: his fine presence, his taste for luxury, his knowledge of French and Italian, made him stand out among the uncouth local worthies. A welcome and convenient recruit for the new masters, he became the personal friend of the governor, Count de Marbeuf. He secured a position as assessor in the court at Ajaccio and managed to establish a private practice as well. Above all, he contrived to have his claims to noble rank officially recognized. This entitled him to the benefactions of His Most Christian Majesty; several of his children—Joseph, Napoleon, Lucien, Eliza—were to be educated in various schools at the King's expense. Even Joseph Fesch, Letizia's half-brother, was not forgotten: he went to Aix to study for the priesthood. His unobtrusive virtues and the grace of his nephew Napoleon were to make him an Archbishop of Lyon, Primate of Gaul, and a cardinal.

The royal bounty was sorely needed. The Buonapartes, though "reputed nobles and patricians for two hundred years", had never been rich. The combined estate of the clan, ably and parsimoniously managed by Uncle Lucciano Buonaparte, archdeacon at Ajaccio, was modest; much of it was tied up in complicated and interminable litigations. If Letizia was thrifty—and thrifty she remained when her son was the new Charlemagne—Carlo was extravagant. His begging expeditions to Versailles were not fruitless, but he also brought back from Paris twelve embroidered suits for himself. The family was increasing faster than the means of support: eight of his thirteen children survived their father.

On 1 January, 1779, Carlo Buonaparte took his two elder sons, Joseph and Napoleon, to the College of Autun, reputed to be among the best in France. Joseph, taller, handsomer, by no means a fool, but of an easy good

nature that verged on indolence, was intended for an
ecclesiastical career; Napoleon, who at the age of nine
had already asserted his fiery temper, was to become a
soldier. After a few months at Autun, improving his
command of French, he proceeded to Brienne, where he
had been granted a scholarship.

Brienne was one of the twelve schools recently selected by Saint-Germain, Minister of War, to serve as
military academies for young noblemen. With a strong
accent on *noblemen*: it was Saint-Germain who, in a
famous ordinance, had hermetically sealed the officers'
corps against commoners. Régimes harden as death closes
upon them: under Louis XVI, Vauban could not have
become a marshal of France.

In spite of its martial purpose, the school was run by a
religious order, the Minims, with a few lay assistants.
The curriculum was practical, free from the emphasis
that for two hundred years the Jesuits had placed on
Latin, rhetoric, and drawing-room manners. The material
conditions were austere, but not unduly harsh. Only one
feature strikes us as unnatural: for the whole six years
of the course the boys were not allowed to go home.
Napoleon was visited only twice: by his father and
mother in 1782, by his father and his younger brother
Lucien in 1784. He was no prodigy and no dunce. He
gave a good account of himself in mathematics; his
dancing was of the poorest; to the end his handwriting
remained gloriously illegible.

Torn from all home associations, he found little solace
in comradeship. He was not sent to Coventry; but, under-
sized, thin and sallow, speaking French with a ludicrous
accent, he was branded as different. Boys can be cruel
little snobs. Half the cadets were the sons of impoverished
gentlemen and were supported by the King's bounty; but
they realized that, among the poor, he was a pauper.

Few of them belonged to the higher nobility; but they did not conceal their scorn for the "patrician" from a remote province recently bought like a piece of real estate and rumoured to be half savage.

The lonely boy became an ardent reader. He devoured the masterpieces of antiquity, particularly the historians, and those of France's great century: his romantic, almost Byronic dreams were cast in a severely classical mould. Throughout his career we shall find in his style sonorous echoes of Corneille, and in his spirit the long shadow of Plutarch. As he was not welcome among the French, his boyish will-to-power took a Corsican turn. He became a fierce island patriot; he hated the oppressors of his people, and worshipped the local demigod, Paoli. Perhaps there was in this attitude a secret rebellion against the turncoat, the collaborationist, the father whom, in all sincerity, he professed to admire and love.

Napoleon had first been intended for the navy, but was shifted to the army. He chose the artillery: in that highly technical branch, brains had a better chance. After an examination he and four others were selected to enter the great military school in Paris. In keeping with Gabriel's stately architecture, the cadets were treated like officers and gentlemen. They lived in a luxury that Napoleon had never known, and was not to know again for another decade. After only one year of study (30 October, 1784, to 28 October, 1785) he was graduated, ranking forty-second out of fifty-eight. Just ahead of him was Phélippeaux, another alumnus of Brienne, who was to defeat him at Acre and perhaps deflect his career. The boy, just over sixteen, was gazetted second lieutenant in the regiment of La Fère.

Meanwhile Carlo Buonaparte, tortured by cancer of the stomach, had gone as a last hope to Montpellier, a medical centre of ancient renown, and had died there on 24 February, 1785. He left his family in a situation full of elusive promises and desperate embarrassments. The estate, in spite of Carlo's tireless solicitations and Uncle Lucciano's management, was tangled up as usual. Joseph (b. 1768) was changing his course from the Church to the army. Lucien (b. 1775), on the contrary, was giving up Brienne for the Seminary at Aix. Both moves were to prove abortive. Eliza (b. 1777) had the best prospects: she had been admitted to Saint-Cyr, the school created by Mme de Maintenon for the daughters of the impoverished aristocracy, whence she was expected to emerge at twenty with the accomplishments of a gentlewoman, a munificent dowry of three thousand francs, and a trousseau. Louis (b. 1778), Pauline (b. 1780), Caroline (b. 1782), and Jerome (b. 1784) were left under the care of the widow, on tenuous and problematic resources.

Although Napoleon, respectful of Corsican tradition, never challenged Joseph's right as the eldest, he had already assumed, *de facto,* the leadership of the clan. He disapproved of his brothers' changes of plans, speaking in the authoritative tones of a world-wise uncle. He took his responsibility seriously: within a quarter of a century, he had found thrones for most of the brood.

But, for all his family concerns, he was first of all, naturally enough, a spirited youngster entering upon the career that he loved. At the pinnacle, he was to remember with fondness the golden days when "he had the honour of being a second lieutenant of artillery". He was sent to Valence, on the Rhône, some sixty miles south of Lyon, where a detachment of his regiment was stationed. He had to go through the drill of the private, the corporal, and the sergeant before he assumed his duties as an officer: the old army believed in apprenticeship rather than in theoretical learning.

Too earnest and too poor for social pleasures, he read more avidly than ever. This time, in the sultry twilight of the ancient régime, he absorbed the political writers: Montesquieu, Mably, Raynal. He was, like most of his contemporaries, steeped in Rousseau. Both young upstarts did reshape the world; both were conscious of their native power, in contrast with their humble standing and the indifference of society; both felt the melancholy that is bred by moral solitude; in both tumultuous minds there were vast dreams not fully under the control of classical reason. Napoleon, aware of the kinship, once wondered whether it would have been better for the world if he and Rousseau had never lived.

Napoleon was not to enjoy for long the studious leisure of a peacetime, small-town garrison. During the next seven years his movements were complicated and at times unaccountable. With revolution in the air, army discipline had grown very lax. Napoleon was on leave for longer periods than on active service. Much of his time he spent in Corsica playing ambiguous politics; part of the rest he was in Paris begging for an extension of his furlough. Ill health, bad weather, anything would serve as an excuse. As a rule, he managed to escape disciplinary measures and to collect most of his back pay. He was not finally dismissed for persistent insubordination until the eve of his becoming commander-in-chief. This is the most obscure and not the least paradoxical chapter in his bewildering career.

He went back to Corsica in September 1786 for the first time in seven years and nine months. On account of a war scare with Prussia (August 1787), all officers were recalled to their posts. But, without tarrying at Valence, Napoleon went on to Paris and was granted a new leave to attend the Estates of Corsica. He arrived in Ajaccio on 1 January, 1788. Joseph, after taking his law degree at Pisa like their father, joined him for a few weeks. In June, Napoleon left to rejoin his unit, now at Auxonne in Burgundy; and for a miracle, he was to stay there for fifteen months.

The mob and the soldiery had caught the fever of July 1789: as an echo of Bastille Day, there was rioting in the placid little town. But by 20 July the officers had restored discipline. Napoleon's political opinions suffered many changes, but he never swerved in his horror of anarchy. Unruly at heart, he craved material order. As late as March 1815 he shuddered and shrank when he was deliriously hailed by the populace. In September 1789 he was off to Corsica again.

With the Revolution the political climate of the island had changed altogether. Corsica, like Alsace, had not grown French through a slow maturing process: although not disloyal, both considered themselves semi-alien. Both were born anew and made one with the French people, in the spirit of liberty. Napoleon, who, in his own mind, had always posed as a lover of freedom, accepted at once the Principles of 1789, while many of his fellow officers were hesitating, or even preparing to desert. In France, Paoli was hailed as a hero and a martyr of the people's cause. On the motion of Mirabeau, he was allowed to return from exile, and he was given the rank of lieutenant-general. The National Assembly received him in triumph. But in his long absence he had learned nothing and forgotten nothing. He was for Corsica first, for Corsica alone. He was ready to accept membership in the French Commonwealth, but on his own terms. Rather than submit to orders from Paris, he would place his country under a British protectorate. Now the Revolution, in the name of "Liberty", was sweeping away all provincial "liberties" as survivals of the Gothic ages. There was from the first a misunderstanding between Paoli and the French

Revolutionists: Napoleon and Joseph were mobbed as Jacobins. Soon after he landed at Bastia, the old hero, whom his people called Babbo (Daddy), was elected President. Pardonably, he welcomed with coolness the sons of the turncoat Carlo.

So, early in 1791, Napoleon, somewhat crestfallen, returned to Auxonne. This time, in order to relieve his mother, he took with him his brother Louis, of whom he was very fond and who was showing delusive promise. He tutored the lad, and for his sake had to deny himself every luxury. The regiment moved back to Valence. Incorrigibly, and over his colonel's opposition, Napoleon wangled another leave for Corsica. For him, as for the whole country, 1792 was a year of inextricable confusion. For outstaying his leave, he was regarded as an *émigré* and forfeited his French commission. In Corsica he got himself elected lieutenant-colonel of volunteers; but he was openly at odds with Paoli, now full master of the island. On Easter Day he made a futile attempt to seize Ajaccio. In May he left for Paris, frustrated, his standing dubious, his outlook dim.

On 20 June he saw the mob invade the royal palace of the Tuileries. The King, who, since his abortive flight to Varennes, thought of himself as a prisoner and a martyr, offered no resistance; he even donned the red cap. *'Che coglione!'*—What a weak fool!—exclaimed the young soldier. But the great war had started; it was to last until 1815. All officers who had not emigrated were welcomed back. No embarrassing questions were pressed: Napoleon received his arrears of pay and was promoted to a captaincy. He was still in Paris on 10 August, when the Tuileries Palace was stormed again. This time the throne collapsed altogether. Napoleon and Eliza (Saint-Cyr had just been suppressed) lived through the days of September, when bands of ruffians, drunk with "preternatural suspicion", massacred the aristocrats who had been rounded up in the prisons, a short, thorough way with security risks.

Back in Ajaccio by 15 October, Napoleon was appointed commander of the National Guards. Two expeditions against Sardinia failed: French sailors and Paolist soldiers came to blows. In April and May 1793 Napoleon made other attempts to capture Ajaccio. He had not yet formally broken with Paoli; but the hero of independence, fiercely denounced by the young firebrand Lucien Buonaparte, was outlawed by the Convention in April 1793. This time the breach was final. Captured by the Paolists, Napoleon managed to escape. The whole family fled to France after melodramatic adventures. Their house was wrecked and looted by the Corsican patriots.

Paoli, hard pressed, had to call in the British in 1794 and to acknowledge the sovereignty of George III. But England was not deeply interested. Finding Paoli difficult, she did not leave him at the head of affairs. In 1796 the island was recaptured by the French. Babbo Paoli was again a refugee in London, where he died obscurely in 1807. The Corsican chapter of Napoleon's history was closed. He saw his native shores again in 1799, on his way back from Egypt, and he called a number of Corsicans into his personal service. But he had out-soared the small, fiery island.

Mme Letizia and her brood had reached Toulon, and then Marseille, where, as French "loyalists", they received a small subsidy from the government. Napoleon was reinstated in the regular army and promoted to major. He seemed wholly committed to the party in power, loosely known as the Jacobins. He wrote an able pamphlet, *The Supper at Beaucaire*, in defence of their policies. He took part in an operation against the counter-revolutionists at Avignon. One of his protectors was Augustin Robespierre, brother of the Dictator, Maximilien.

In that climatic year 1793, while France was struggling against Europe on every frontier, the west— Vendée, Normandy, Brittany was ablaze. Lyon, the second city, was in rebellion, and Toulon, the one great naval base on the Mediterranean, welcomed the British and Spanish fleets (28 August, 1793). Carteaux, a painter of modest fame turned amateur strategist, was feebly attempting to recapture Toulon. Napoleon served under him with rage in his heart. Carteaux was superseded by Dugommier, a soldier who knew his trade. The artillery was placed under General du Teil, a capable officer whose brother had been much impressed by Lieutenant Buonaparte at Auxonne; and so the young major had his chance at last. He did not conquer Toulon single-handed; but he had an eagle's eye for key positions and he used his batteries to best advantage. There is no reason to doubt the commendation of General du Teil: "He has abundant knowledge, with intelligence to match it; and bravery unsurpassed." "From the sublime to the ridiculous", to use a famous Napoleonic phrase: while gathering laurels he also caught the itch, which was to annoy him for many years. Toulon was captured on 19 December, 1793. There were massive reprisals: Napoleon, a subordinate, was not able to check them.

The path of glory seemed clear at last. The twenty-four-year-old was promoted to brigadier-general, sent for a tour of inspection on the Italian front, entrusted with a secret mission to Genoa. His plan for an offensive in Italy, transmitted by Augustin Robespierre, was approved by the authorities in Paris, even though the best military heads were unconvinced. An important command seemed within his reach. Then came a sharp set-back. He had

been swimming with the Jacobin tide; and on the 9th
Thermidor[1] (23 July, 1794), Maximilien Robespierre was
overthrown. A few days later (9 August), Napoleon was
suspended and placed under arrest.

He had not been compromised in political intrigues,
however, and he was soon released; but the momentum
of his ascent seemed broken. The Italian offensive was
deferred. An expedition for the reconquest of Corsica
(4—14 March, 1795) was thwarted by the British fleet.
Napoleon was again without a definite job; and again, on
2 May, he started for Paris, where so many of his battles
were fought. He haunted the lobbies of the Convention
and of the War Office: a disquieting figure, shabby,
almost ludicrous, with flashes of impressive pride and
with a record as mottled and disconcerting as his appearance—many fumbling lunges and a single very creditable
achievement.

He was given a stop-gap assignment in the Topo-
graphical Section; but what he wanted was an active
command, and in a field of his own choosing. Aubry,
the man in charge of staff appointments, was himself a
disgruntled artillerist: he thought the ambitions of
the fledgling general preposterous. He offered him a
brigade of infantry in the Army of the West. Napoleon
had no stomach for that treacherous Vendean warfare:
what glory could be reaped from obscure skirmishes with
fanatical peasants? He declined the offer, at first under
the plea of ill health. He was granted a short respite;
when that expired, his name was struck off the list of
generals on active duty. On the same day as the news
of his dismissal, he received the official offer of a mission

1 By decree of the Convention, the year I of the Republic began
on September 22, 1792. The months were named: Vendémiaire,
Brumaire, Frimaire; Nivôse, Pluviôse, Ventôse; Germinal, Floréal,
Prairial Messidor, Thermidor, Fructidor. This calendar remained
in official use until January 1, 1806.

to Turkey to reorganize the Sultan's artillery. On the eve of the Revolution, he had thought of a career in India: this was a second glimpse of that fabulous East which held for him such a romantic fascination. The plan fell through; the dream remained.

Another will-o'-the-wisp flitted through Napoleon's life. When the Buonapartes were in Marseille they became acquainted with the Clary family: a solid fortune, made out of silk and soap. There was an exchange of services. Handsome Joseph won the hand of Julie Clary; and it looked as though Napoleon intended to claim her little sister Désirée as his bride. Her heart was his: we have touching letters from sweet eighteen to the hero of Toulon. How deeply the hero had committed himself we do not know. M. Clary is reported to have said: "One Buonaparte in the family is enough." The plain fact is that Napoleon, undaunted by his slender purse and dubious prospects, had made his way among the victors of Thermidor: a society not renowned for squeamishness, but dazzling to the young adventurer. In that glitter the endearing young charms of poor little Désirée faded from his memory. She married Charles Bernadotte, a vigorous, astute soldier whom Napoleon never liked or trusted, but whom he made a marshal of France and Prince of Pontecorvo. The Swedes, in 1810, chose Bernadotte as their Prince Royal; and Désirée Clary died as Queen of Sweden in 1860.

Then came Napoleon's supreme chance. Thermidor had left France in material and moral chaos. If Robespierre was the Tyrant, he was also the Incorruptible: with the reign of Terror, the reign of Virtue came to an abrupt end. Many of the Thermidorians had been terrorists—some of them out of terror. Most of them were corrupt; above all, their chief, Barras, *Rois des Pourris* (king of rottenness). That sorry crew tried to preserve its precarious power for safety and for loot against a resurgence of Jacobinism on the one hand, against a frank and thorough royalist reaction on the other. For their own protection, they added to the new constitution a clause requiring that two-thirds of the representatives in the future assemblies should be chosen from the expiring and discredited Convention.

So Thermidor was to be saddled for years upon the new régime. The scandal was too great: the "Sections" (the forty-eight wards of Paris) were roused to violent protest. The opposition to the Thermidorian rulers was probably more royalist than republican; but party lines were not sharply drawn. The movement was "retching rather than insurrection". Yet Paris might experience another disastrous "Day": the masses, blindly marching against the Convention, might destroy the last shreds of organized government. The insurgents were short of arms; so were the loyal troops. The Sections had no recognized leaders: the regulars had Menou, who was of two minds, neither very good.

Barras, the natural chief of the Thermidorians, had himself appointed commander-in-chief. But he was aware of his limitations as a military man: he looked round for a professional soldier. The best generals were at the front. Fortunately, he thought of Buonaparte, hungrily prowling for a job. He had met him in "society"; but he had also seen him at Toulon. He turned the work over to him.

The sympathies of Napoleon may well have been with the insurgents: he, too, despised the profiteers of Thermidor. But for him as for Goethe, disorder was the worst of all evils. The government was beneath contempt: still, it was the only government. Besides, he had received no offer from the amorphous discontent of the Sections.

As it was in Toulon, as it was to be almost to the very

end, he saw at a single glance the key to the situation.
Without guns the loose masses could win through their
sheer weight; but they would be powerless against
artillery. Guns were at hand, only a few miles away,
stored in the Sablons Plain: he dispatched Murat the
swift, who seized them in the nick of time. Meanwhile,
he posted the loyal troops at the right points to protect
the Convention—and waited.

There was no organized, concentrated fighting. Some
guns were fired on the quays. There was some shooting
on the steps of the Church of St.-Roch, but there is no
record that Napoleon was present at that point, that he
ordered the firing, or that he considered it decisive. The
"whiff of grapeshot" belongs to Carlyle rather than to
Napoleon. The insurrection was an enormous bubble
that met the sharp point of an iron will. It was not
defeated: it vanished (13 Vendémiaire—5 October,
1795).

Napoleon, "the Sword of Thermidor", was rewarded
at once, and handsomely. On 11 October he was reinstated
in the army as major-general. On 25 October he succeeded
Barras as commander in chief of the Army of the Interior.
The greatest rewards were soon to follow: the hand of
Josephine and, as a wedding gift, the Italian command.

CHAPTER TWO

GENERAL BONAPARTE

REHEARSALS FOR EMPIRE:
ITALY AND EGYPT

1796—1799

WHEN normal life was restored after the Jacobin orgy
of Terror and Virtue, the centre of society was the
drawing-room of Mme Tallien. That superb creature,
daughter of the Spanish banker Cabarrus and divorced
wife of Count de Fontenay, was called, for her beauty
and power, "Our Lady of Thermidor". She had—passively
—contributed to the downfall of the Incorruptible. Young
Tallien, sent by Robespierre to curb the royalist city
of Bordeaux, saw Thérèse and was converted to more
humane ways. He spared her, and thus incurred the
dread accusation of *modérantisme*. He saved himself and
his beloved by leading the attack against the tyrant. He
married her in December 1794. But this was the climax
of his meteoric career. Soon Thérèse became the chief
ornament of Barras's extensive harem. Power as well
as marital happiness slipped from Tallien's hands. His
decline was steady and prolonged. He died, forgotten and
destitute, in 1820.

Mme Tallien, the soul of mercy, helped many victims
of the Terror. In her generous distribution of favours, she
seldom forgot her rake-off. Queen of the Thermidorians,

C

she was, like them, a staunch believer in the profit motive.
When young General Buonaparte found his way into that
demi-monde—titles, glitter, luxury, and no moral
armature—the boon he craved was a very modest one.
His uniform was threadbare, and a parsimonious quartermaster refused to issue cloth for a new one. Mme Tallien
smiled, nodded, and the quartermaster saw the light.
It was in Mme Tallien's circle that Napoleon met
Josephine. Like Tallien with Thérèse, he was subjugated:
one glance, and the hungry young lion was in love.

Josephine Tascher de la Pagerie was born in
Martinique in 1763. In 1779 she married the Comte
Alexandre de Beauharnais. Both families belonged to the
lesser nobility; both sprang from Orléanais; both had
interests in the island: Alexandre was the second son of
the governor. In Paris and Versailles the young pair
enjoyed that "sweetness of living" which, in Talleyrand's
nostalgic words, characterized the last years of the old
régime. Their union, however, was stormy; and a formal
separation was decreed in 1785. Beauharnais espoused
the cause of the Revolution and rose high: as a civilian,
to the presidency of the Assembly; as a soldier, to the
command of an army. But aristocratic transfuges were
constantly under suspicion. Beauharnais, selected as
scapegoat for the fall of Mainz, was arrested and
guillotined. Josephine also was imprisoned and sentenced
to death: she was saved by the 9th Thermidor. She had
two children, Eugene and Hortense, destined to play
conspicuous parts in the grand drama of the Empire.

In 1795, she was among the merriest widows of the
hectic Thermidorian world. She had had a brief affair
with General Hoche; she counted for a while among
Barras's mistresses. In his venomous *Memoirs,* Barras
brands her as cold-hearted, venal, and lascivious:
impressive charges from such a Galahad. Her beauty

could not compare with Mme Tallien's; but she combined to perfection languorous grace and aristocratic refinement. The freshness of youth had already departed: in those days Creoles aged rapidly. But as the Huguenot poet Agrippa d'Aubigné puts it: *"Une rose d'automne est plus qu'une autre exquise"* (what so exquisite as an autumn rose?) Like Queen Jezebel in Racine's *Athaliah,* she knew "how to repair the irreparable outrages of Time". Her dark eyes were lustrous and caressing. Because she had bad teeth, she affected a mysterious, tight-lipped, Mona Lisa smile.

Their meeting was Josephine's Austerlitz: Napoleon was at her mercy. It seems strange that a young man so self-centred and so confident should have been so utterly conquered by a woman six years older than himself, fading, with no solid position, and with a reputation that was not even equivocal. No doubt he was dazzled by her Old Court charm: she provided a link with the fabulous Versailles he had known only from afar. And she had a faint aura of that exoticism which Bernardin de Saint-Pierre's *Paul and Virginia* had made fashionable. Above all, in his austere youth and in his rough military experience, he had been starved of luxury and tenderness, and Josephine offered an admirable imitation of both. A Barras, with his blasé worldly wisdom, could see that both were flimsy and meretricious. But Napoleon was not of the same breed as Barras. There can be no greatness without a touch of naïveté.

How ardent his passion was, his torrid letters from Italy give irrefutable proof. Josephine's hold upon him was not merely that of an experienced harlot: his love for that shallow woman was deep. It withstood time and distance. It was she who first played false. While in Italy, he pretended to be half-blind; on his return from Egypt, he knew everything and forgave everything. This is the finest example of generosity in a ruthlessly egotistic career. Although the expression may sound irreverent, there is genuine sympathy in the Gallic phrase: *"C'est encore comme cocu qu'il est le plus grand"* (it is as a deceived husband that he best reveals his greatness). Nearly twenty years later, at La Malmaison, he could still evoke in the presence of Hortense the graceful phantom of his first and undying love: 'My good Josephine! Certainly the most charming person I ever met . . . a woman through and through. . . .' adding with a rueful smile: 'But her debts! How I used to scold her about them!'

'My *good* Josephine!' Here is the key. She was loose, lazy, cold-hearted, empty-headed: but she possessed the gift of easy kindliness, and she used that slender gift with consummate art. So there arose in France, as in the heart of Napoleon himself, a nebulous but indestructible legend: Josephine, the elusive, yet not wholly deceitful smile of a stiff and frowning régime, Josephine the Eternal Feminine tempering the rigour of the stern hero. In popular imagination it was she who brought Napoleon luck, innocent Marie-Louise who was his evil star.

They were married at night, on 9 March, 1796: in sketchiest fashion, without any religious ceremony. They bridged the gap of years between them: she confessed to twenty-nine instead of thirty-three; he boosted his twenty-seven by eighteen months. She laid vague claims to the riches of the Indies; he proudly admitted that he owned nothing but his cloak and his sword. But, with his already imperial contempt for balanced budgets, he settled upon her an annuity of eighteen thousand francs. In spite of these "castles in Italy", she was not quite sure that Puss-in-Boots, as she had first called her ardent suitor, was a sound investment; but she was flattered by his juvenile storminess; and Barras, who had an eye for business, had advised the match. Three days later, the bridegroom, still drunk with love, was on his way to Italy.

The Italian command has been called a wedding gift, but it was far more. The new five-headed executive, the Directory, had appointed Bonaparte (he had discarded the Italian spelling of his name) without a dissenting vote. He had applied for the assignment; he desired it ardently; he had closely studied the Italian threatre of war, and had sent to headquarters volumes of suggestions and plans. Above all, he had impressed everyone with his coolness and decision in Vendémiaire. Promotion did not wait on seniority in those days.

Highly as the Directors thought of the young general, they were aware that he was untried in large-scale operations. But the Italian campaign was not intended to be the major one. Napoleon's genius, and the luck that followed him almost to the end of his career, completely altered the original picture.

In 1795 Prussia, Spain, Holland, and Tuscany had made peace with the French Republic. Genoa and Venice were neutral. There remained England and, on the Continent, Austria, with Piedmont (Kingdom of Sardinia) as a minor ally. The master of strategy was still Lazare Carnot, the Organizer of Victory. He was the man who in 1793 had welded raw levies into a formidable host, fourteen army corps and twelve hundred thousand men. He had evolved a new method of warfare, swift, tireless, and massive, with which his improvised officers could upset the meticulous chess game of the old tacticians. Practically all of Napoleon's generals were graduates of the Carnot school: he forged the instrument that made the imperial epic possible. Now Carnot planned to impose peace in Vienna itself by sending two armies north of the Alps, one by way of the Main, the other down the Danube. These were entrusted to generals of established

reputation: Jourdan, the victor of Fleurus and Wattignies;
Moreau, known as a careful and efficient commander.
The plan was so good and so obvious that Napoleon was
to borrow it twice, in 1805 and in 1809. The Italian route
on the contrary did not lead straight to Vienna: the
eastern spurs of the Alps would oppose a formidable
obstacle to invasion. This much Austria could guess: she
put her best general, Archduke Charles, in command of
the northern armies. To Italy she sent reinforcements
piecemeal, always "too little and too late".

But Jourdan, who, after his two early victories, was
invariably unlucky, was sharply defeated. Moreau, left
unsupported, had to effect a retreat that has remained
a classic: unbroken, he managed to capture guns and
prisoners from his pursuers. When, after this disastrous
set-back, the Directory picked up Carnot's plan again and
sent two armies over the same routes, one under Moreau,
the other under Hoche, the campaign opened magnificently and came to an abrupt close: for Napoleon, acting
as though he were a sovereign, signed an armistice that
was almost a peace treaty; and the Italian campaign
stood out as a unique and luminous achievement.

'Soldiers! You are destitute: I am leading you into
the richest plains in the world.' These famous words,
though not apocryphal, were perhaps not uttered at the
time; but they admirably express the spirit of Napoleon,
his army, and his government. The Directory, suffering
from a chronic state of bankruptcy, could not bear the
cost of war; on the contrary, it relied upon war to refill
its exchequer, a sieve of the Danaïdes. The Italian
campaign was a *razzia* or looting raid on an epic scale.
The government had misgivings about the airs the young
proconsul was taking on. They sent Saliceti, Kellermann,
Clarke, to keep watch on him or share the command with

him; Napoleon shrugged them away and replied by assuming still more powers. But what could be done with a general who was shipping home gold, jewellery, art treasures, by the cartload? The army contractors grew fat—but they had to provide the goods; the generals were encouraged to line their pockets. Napoleon himself kept loftily clean: his quarry was higher. He merely attended to the needs of his family: Joseph made a fortune as commissary of the armies. The hero himself returned with a paltry three millions.

The details of the military operations have no place in this biographical sketch. But the merest layman is thrilled by the masterly game played by young Bonaparte. He was not to display the same unerring virtuosity again until 1814, in the wonderful and tragic campaign of France; and by that time, no skill would avail any more.

Starting from Nice in April 1796, Napoleon defeated the Austrians at Montenotte, Millesimo, Dego; the Piedmontese at Mondovi. Victor Amadeus, King of Sardina, was compelled to sign an onerous armistice at Cherasco. Then, turning on the Austrian commander Beaulieu, Napoleon crossed the Po at Piacenza, the Adda at Lodi (there it was that his soldiers first called him "the Little Corporal"), and entered as a conqueror the queen city of Lombardy, Milan.

He was hailed by the Milanese as a liberator. Perhaps it was their enthusiasm that focused his destiny. He felt himself no longer a mere general, but a being apart, a demigod commanding the devotion of multitudes. He did not reflect—neither did posterity—that it was not his victory that the Italians were celebrating, but the defeat of the Austrians. We realize now that Napoleon was like a young heir coming into a vast heritage. He stood for France; the splendour of the Grand Monarch, the charm of the Paris salons, the exhilaration of the Enlightenment, the immense hope raised by the storming of the Bastille, the miracle of Carnot's victories. The coming of the French seemed to herald a new heaven and a new earth. That treasure of good will, so clearly manifested when, on 15 May, 1796, Milan tumultuously cheered the victor, Napoleon was to grab as his own—and to squander. The victory, material and moral, was dazzling but precarious, as the greatest of Napoleon's victories were destined to be. Less than a fortnight after his triumphal entry into Milan, Lombardy rose against him; he ordered Pavia to be pillaged as a lesson.

By the end of May he had driven Beaulieu into the Tyrol; in June he had laid siege to the key fortress, Mantua. Then he had to face a more redoubtable adversary, Field Marshal Count Würmser. For a while the situation looked ominous. But Würmser in his turn was hurled back at Castiglione; when he returned, he was routed at Bassano and had to seek refuge in Mantua, which, after a set-back, Napoleon was besieging again. All sorties were repulsed, and on 2 February, 1797, the renowned old marshal had to capitulate. Another army under Alvinzi was beaten at Arcola and Rivoli.

At last Archduke Charles assumed command against Napoleon. But by that time Austria no longer enjoyed numerical superiority. Charles had to abandon the line of the Tagliamento. He was pursued into the mountains of Carinthia. An armistice was signed at Leoben on 17 April; it served as a basis for the triumphant peace of Campoformio (17 October, 1797).

Triumphant, yet equivocal. It was only another move in a protracted game. The French at Klagenfurt were still a long, hard way from Vienna; and if Austria was exhausted, so was France. But this was the cynical age that had seen the three partitions of Poland. Prussia at Basel and Austria at Campoformio yielded so much only because they expected to recoup themselves at the expense of their lesser allies and of the neutrals. In dynastic Europe the desires of the population counted for nothing: "souls" were neatly balanced in complicated deals. Whatever may have been the early ideal of the French Revolution—a crusade for democracy—by 1797 the Directory and Napoleon were playing exactly the same ruthless game of Frederick, Catherine, and Maria-Theresa, a blend of force and fraud.

Only they played that game, like novices drunk with their own luck, far more recklessly than their fore-runners. The pace grew furious. From 1797 to 1812, republics were created and abolished (it was in 1797 that Genoa and Venice ceased to be, two commercial oligarchies stiff with age and tarnished splendour), grand duchies and kingdoms carved out and suppressed—Berg, Etruria, Westphalia, Warsaw—by a flash of the sword and a stroke of the pen. It was a most exciting game; only it never was quite real. The whole of middle Europe was a teeming chaos of tiny principalities, bishoprics, free cities, which were medieval ghosts. The people were bewildered and indifferent. The dynasties stood for no principle, but gambled or fought for the spoils. If Europe had not been such an array of obsolete incongruities, the fantastic scene-shiftings done by the Directory and Napoleon would have been inconceivable.

Meanwhile the young conqueror had imposed his will on Parma, Modena, and the Pope. Resting from his labours, he was now holding court at the castle of Mombello, near Milan. The whole family was summoned to bask in the sunshine of his glory: Mme Letizia, Eliza, Pauline, Caroline, Joseph, Louis, Eugene. There the Corsican felt himself king, as Louis XVI had never been: king by the divine right of genius and destiny. The new Minister of Foreign Affairs, Talleyrand, wrote to him not as to a general of the Republic, but as to a prince whose favour was to be courted. Josephine graced the marvellous scene. She had offered many excuses for not joining him, but she had yielded at last to his ardent entreaties. To be sure, she brought in her train, with a vague staff appointment, young Hippolyte Charles, whom she found less heroic, but far more amusing, than her legitimate Puss-in-Boots.

Campoformio was to be followed by a congress at Rastatt for the general resettlement of Europe. Napoleon was appointed minister plenipotentiary; but it soon became evident to him that there was no genuine desire for peace on either side, and after a few days (November-December 1797) he returned to Paris. The Congress was to drag on uneasily for over a year and then break up when hositilities were resumed.

In Paris, Napoleon received a hero's welcome. Everything at home was confusion and corruption. Directory and Assemblies were plotting feebly and indecisively against each other. *Coups d'état* had become a routine political method. On the 18th Fructidor (4 September, 1797), the Directors had borrowed from Napoleon a sword, General Augereau, to cut their eternal Gordian knot once more. Napoleon's exactions in Italy had at any rate been profitable to France; in the miasmatic atmosphere of the political world his victories came with healing in their wings. Wherever he appeared, ministers and directors faded into insignificance. And—supreme coquetry of the victorious soldier—he affected to prize above all other rewards his election to the learned Institute of France as a mathematician.

But he did not see his way to power yet. As a general, in spite of his miraculous achievements, he was still only first among his peers. Hoche, the greatest of all, was dead;

but Moreau, Masséna, Desaix, Kléber, or Joubert, guided by expert politicians, could have barred his way. He was bored and restless. He inspected the Army of the West, intended to strike at England; but he saw that the chances of a direct attack were slim. So he yielded to his dream and to his devouring gambling instinct: he would try his luck in the "gorgeous East", fountain-head of legends, religions, and empires.

He had already given the subject serious thought in Italy. He had wrested from Venice the Ionian Islands— Corfu, Cephalonia, and Zante—as stepping-stones to the land of wonders. He had sent the government a memorandum about Malta. The thought was in the air: on 3 July, 1797, just before he became Minister of Foreign Affairs, Talleyrand had read at a meeting of the Institute a paper on the necessity for new colonies, and he had singled out Egypt as a favourable field. So the Egyptian campaign was decided, and the expedition set forth from Toulon on 19 May, 1798.

The whole enterprise was so preposterous that it remains an enigma. The Directory and Napoleon must have known that they could not wrench permanent control of the sea from England. France had good sailors and ample materials for building a fleet; but the officers' corps had been practically destroyed by the Revolution. This was true also of the land forces; but there new methods had given France the advantage, and there was nothing of the kind in naval matters. Privateering and occasional raids were still possible, not large-scale operations. Even if the French did reach Egypt, they would still be separated from India, their strategic goal, by three thousand miles of desert or sea. They could not throttle British trade: the main route was by way of the Cape. The blindest could see that the peace of Campoformio was precarious. How a government could send its best general and its best army overseas on such a wild adventure passes imagination. The desire to get rid of an embarrassing and all too popular hero would hardly justify such a suicidal move. In addition, the ever-indigent Directory could not afford such a costly enterprise: the treasury of Berne and the churches of Rome had to be rifled to meet the initial outlay.

If the consent of the Directory remains incomprehensible, Napoleon's decision is intelligible enough in terms not of strategy but of psychology. There was in his nature a strange dualism that explains both his repeated failures and his undying prestige. He was a blend of severe realistic common sense served by an unequalled efficiency, and an untamable imagination. He stood, like his whole epoch, in the mingling lights of classical reason and romantic wonder. He loved mathematics and he revelled in Ossian. All great men must be guided by a dream. But in the case of Napoleon, there was a hiatus between his gigantic unsubstantial visions and the sharply practical means of execution. The Egyptian campaign was swiftly and admirably organized. It included a notable team of scientists, scholars, and engineers. When it left Toulon—four hundred vessels, from the stately *Orient* down, carrying fifty-four thousand men—it offered a most imposing spectacle; and lo, from the very first, it was a mirage.

Repeatedly Napoleon spoke of his "star", his miraculous luck. Nelson, the Napoleon of the sea, might have defeated the French armada the moment it started out, but a storm had compelled him to seek harbour. Once the French caught sight of him, but he failed to see them, and they slipped by. He was at Alexandria a few days ahead of them, but sailed away again on a wild-goose chase. When the inevitable finally happened and the French fleet was destroyed in the bay of Aboukir (Battle of the Nile, 1 August, 1798), the French, who had landed a month before, were already firmly established in Egypt. On their way, they had captured impregnable Malta from its knights without a fight: "thankful to find someone there to hand them the keys".

Egypt, nominally part of the Ottoman Empire, was governed, or rather exploited, by a loose military oligarchy, the Mameluke beys. France would claim to act in the name of the Sultan, and to suppress the unruly praetorians who had usurped his power. Talleyrand was to go to Constantinople to secure the agreement of the Porte; but he found it more sensible to remain at home. The flimsy pretext, however, was duly invoked, and when the troops landed, the Turkish flag was flown by the side of the French. Turkey, unconvinced, declared war on France, and struck an alliance with Russia and England.

Alexandria fell, and then Cairo. The Mamelukes, a medieval cavalry, were defeated; and "from the heights of the Pyramids, forty centuries [rather *blasés* with the pageantry of invasion] contemplated the French Army". With his customary swiftness and energy, Napoleon organized a protectorate. It was intelligent, but it did not work. The population did not take very seriously his profession of Islamic piety. They soon found out that the old taxes, under new names and more stringently collected, were fully as crushing as before. After a few weeks of hopeful waiting, Cairo rebelled. The insurgents were mowed down with Napoleonic efficiency.

After the Battle of the Nile, Napoleon was trapped in his new conquest. He was sovereign indeed: if he was cut off from reinforcements and supplies, he was free from interference. He was Sultan of Egypt more literally than he had been King of Italy at Mombello. He was disenchanted: Egypt was his own, but a poor thing.

Instead of fabled wealth, reality offered abject poverty.

Among the news that capriciously filtered in from France, the most indisputable related to Josephine's flightiness: Hippolyte Charles, among others, was in the ascendant again. Napoleon consoled himself with Mme Fourès, who had stowed herself away with the army under a man's uniform. For the sake of morality, the husband was shipped back to France. He was captured by the English, who, duly informed of the situation, returned him to Napoleon: there is a dry quality about British humour. Pauline Fourès ("Bellilote") was sprightly, and Napoleon would have made her his permanent sultana if she had given him a child. She failed, and disappeared from history. Her second husband rose to high positions under the Empire.

Napoleon decided to occupy Syria. The reasons are not clear; the results are unequivocal. He took El Arish, Gaza, Jaffa; there he had twelve hundred prisoners of war shot because they were an encumbrance: not cruel by nature, he was free from squeamishness. He reached Acre; but Sir Sidney Smith had already landed forces there, including Napoleon's schoolmate Phélippeaux. The French had to give up the siege and trudge their painful way back to Egypt. A last ghastly touch was added to that nightmarish retreat: they were stricken with the plague. On 14 July, 1799, Napoleon was back in Cairo. On 25 July he thrust back a Turkish army that had landed at Aboukir. He was Napoleon still, but what now?

So far as he was concerned, the game was up. To remain as the ever-threatened sultan of a poverty-stricken and beleaguered Egypt did not tempt him in the least. Kléber, whom he planned to leave in command, was not informed of his intentions. On 22 August Napoleon sneaked aboard the frigate *Muiron*; he set sail the next day.

His star was still with him: his nimble little ships—
two frigates and a few smaller vessels—eluded the British
cruisers. He stopped for a few days in Corsica, landed in
the bay of Fréjus.

His sole justification for returning was the desperate
plight of France, of which he had been apprised by the
British themselves. Russia, which for seven years had
been inactive in the west, had at last joined the coalition.
It now included Great Britain, Austria, Naples, Portugal,
and the Ottoman Empire, the most formidable array
France had ever had to face. By an ironical twist of fate,
France had been saved just before Napoleon landed:
through the victories of Brune at Bergen (19 September)
and of Masséna at Zürich (26 September). This failed
to affect public opinion: Napoleon was hailed with
delirious joy, and his progress from Fréjus to Paris was
a triumph. Others might win battles: it was believed
that he alone could achieve peace. Above all, France
wanted a strong man to sweep away Thermidorian mis-
rule; and the Thermidorians wanted a strong man to con-
solidate their profits. It happened that the same man
could serve both turns.

CHAPTER THREE

THE MAN OF THE HOUR

BONAPARTE FIRST CONSUL

1799—1802

NAPOLEON'S seizure of absolute power on the 18th and 19th Brumaire (9-10 November, 1799) was not a mere *coup de force,* a simple, brutal act, but an imbroglio worthy of Figaro himself. As in Beaumarchais's comedies, the plot grew so tangled at one point that the protagonists must have wondered: *"Qui trompe-t-on ici?"* (which side is being duped?) At the crucial moment Napoleon broke down, and his triumph was a fluke. But there was more than mere luck in his sweeping victory. Blunder as he might, no other contender had so many trumps in his hand or up his sleeve. For fully two years he was literally the man of the hour. But after he had seized control, he managed to keep it for fifteen.

After a whole decade of revolutions and seven years of war, conditions in France offered a sharp contrast. With a fertile soil and a long tradition of hard work the country had survived all convulsions. Much dead wood had been removed; many fresh energies released. Lafayette, returning from exile, was struck with the prosperity of the land. But the new society had not yet found its balance. The subconscious unity that comes from immemorial habit had been shaken even before 1789;

the tense unity that is the result of a great common purpose had been shattered when Robespierre was overthrown. The people were not exactly dissatisfied with
existing conditions; they wanted neither a return to the
old régime nor a new social order; what they desired was
a sense of permanency. The situation, political, economic,
and military, was confused rather than desperate. France
yearned for tranquillity at home and peace abroad. As the
constituted authorities could achieve neither, the people
saw no relief but in "the *coup d'état* to end all *coups
d'état*".

Thermidor had been the triumph of plutocracy.
Siéyès's dictum had come true: the Third Estate—that is,
the moneyed bourgeoisie—was everything, the aristocracy very little, the common people nothing. The
Revolution was ended, the rule of the middle class established. But thanks to five years of mismanagement, the
new régime was still open to challenge. Socialism, which
is implicit in Rousseauism,[1] had made its first appearance
in modern politics with the conspiracy of Babeuf—Caius
Gracchus Babeuf, for this was the age of pseudo-
classicism. Radical measures had been proposed: a return
to price-fixing, a levy on capital. The financiers were
definitely alarmed; among them Ouvrard (1770-1846),
who was to remain for many decades a power behind the
scenes. For constitutional forms the moneyed interests
cared very little; they were concerned with the essence:
the divine right of property.

The instability of the régime was felt most keenly by
those at the top. They knew that their fall was imminent,
and eager to safeguard their own gains, the shrewdest
among them were plotting against their own government.

[1] "The earth belongs to none, its fruit to all" (*Discourse on
the Origin of Inequality*). In Proudhon's blunter terms: "Property
is theft."

D

The Directors, in the last phase, were Barras, Siéyès, Roger-Ducos, Gohier, and General Moulins. The last two were honest republicans, and easy to hoodwink. Roger-Ducos was the partner, or shadow, of Siéyès. The key men were Siéyès and Barras.

Both had their origins in the old privileged orders: Barras was a viscount, Siéyès a priest. Both had abjured their former allegiances and were committed to the only realistic cause: money. There were great differences between them. Barras was first of all a voluptuary, Siéyès a theorist. Barras, in power for five years, had had his fill; Siéyès felt that his hour had come at last. In the early stages of the Revolution his famous pamphlet *What Is the Third Estate?* had won him renown for political profundity; a few oracular speeches and unplumbed depths of silence had confirmed it. During the Terror, he had ducked under. Questioned later, he answered: *'J'ai vécu,'* (I saved my skin). Now he had emerged again; he had been successful in a mission to Prussia, and had been made a Director. It was time for him to give France the perfect constitution he had evolved in his years of silent meditation. For his great purpose, he needed an instrument, and one of higher quality than a rough soldier like Augereau. He had thought of Joubert, but Joubert was killed at Novi on 15 August, 1799; and of Moreau, but that great and cautious strategist, hampered by a combination of loyalty and timidity, did not respond to his advances. Then Napoleon landed, and Siéyès understood that no one would have a chance against him. So, not without misgivings, he decided to employ Napoleon.

Napoleon had hopes of his own: he had been king in Italy, sultan in Egypt, and was ready, not to share power with others, but to grasp it for himself alone. As he had a vast, loose following, but no organized party, he needed a friend within the gates. His natural ally would have been Barras, as in Vendémiaire; but Barras was too sceptical and too weary for a bold adventure. Napoleon's best chance, perhaps his only chance, was to co-operate with Siéyès. Thus the theorist and the man of action, profoundly disliking and distrusting each other, struck a secret alliance. Their mutual hostility was outwardly preserved as a blind. In public, they met only to glare at each other; in the wings, they perfected their plans for a peaceful political comedy.

We find engaged in this conspiracy two fascinating characters without scruples, fear, or mercy, who were to work with Napoleon so closely and against him so effectively that they are inseparable from his destiny. These were Talleyrand and Fouché. It might be said that from 1800 to 1815 France was ruled by a triumvirate in which the splendid central personage was not invariably the most powerful. It was Talleyrand who, as an honest broker, brought Napoleon and Siéyès together. It was he also who secured the retirement of Barras. Rumour had it that he came to Barras with a heavy bribe, provided by Ouvrard; Barras was so eager to quit that he did not even sell out; Talleyrand, surprised and delighted, pocketed the money. Fouché, as Minister of Police, had a hundred eyes and closed them obstinately to the obvious Bonaparte-Siéyès conspiracy. In compensation, he invented a horrific Jacobin plot, which was to serve as a pretext for emergency measures. After the *coup d'état* had been effected, he helped manipulate public opinion, and he saw to it that order was not disturbed in Paris. It is odd to see the Man on Horseback force his way to power aided and escorted by three rather dubious ecclesiastics: Talleyrand had been Bishop of Autun, Siéyès an abbé, Fouché a tonsured and cassocked Oratorian brother.

The preparations proceeded with admirable efficiency. Young Lucien Bonaparte, who loved political strife as his brother loved the battlefield, was elected President of the Lower House, or Council of the Five Hundred, where republicanism was still very strong. With a show of bluff cordiality, Napoleon won over General Lefebvre, commander of the Paris division.[1] Lefebvre cried enthusiastically: 'Let's throw those prattlers into the river!' With Moreau, Napoleon used deference and professions of republican orthodoxy. Moreau was so far duped that he agreed to keep watch on Gohier and Moulins, the two Directors who were not in the plot. According to plan, the Councils resolved that, in view of the Jacobin menace, they would remove to Saint-Cloud; and they entrusted General Bonaparte with all the necessary measures for the defence of the Republic. This was the 18th Brumaire, 9 November, 1799.

On the next day the Councils met at Saint-Cloud, a royal palace a few miles west of Paris, destroyed by fire in 1870. No hitch so far; but it is a risk to let a night intervene between the two acts of a *coup d'état*. The Upper House, quaintly called the Council of Ancients, was well disposed; but even there Napoleon's forcible and incoherent ranting made a bad impression. When he moved to the Council of Five Hundred, which was meeting in the Orangery, he was hailed with violent denunciations: 'Down with the dictator! Death to the tyrant! Outlaw him!' It was with these cries that Robespierre had been silenced and overthrown on the 9th Thermidor. Napoleon had a cool mind and no lack of physical courage; yet in that unfamiliar storm he lost his nerve, stammered, and

---

[1] Lefebvre was an old trooper who had married a laundress. In 1808 they were to blossom out as Duke and Duchess of Danzig. The Duchess, vivid, fearless, with a gift of tangy picturesque speech, remains a favourite character in French folk-lore as *Madame Sans-Gêne*.

fumbled. The whole plot seemed in danger of collapsing. It was the civilians, young and old, Lucien and Siéyès, who retrieved the day. 'They outlaw you?' said Siéyès, 'outlaw them!' Lucien, in his capacity as President, declared that the Assembly was terrorized by assassins (Arena was seen brandishing a penknife), and officially requested the troops, massed in readiness, to restore order. Murat came in first and gave the sharp command: 'Throw them out of the windows!' Leclerc followed and mopped up. Leclerc was the husband of Pauline; Murat was soon to be rewarded with the hand of Caroline; with Lucien in the key position, the 19th Brumaire was a cosy brotherly affair. Soon the long red robes of the Five Hundred were seen flitting through the park.

The Directory had vanished, lamentable and unlamented. The Ancients registered the fact. A few representatives of the Five Hundred—some fifty—were rounded up and gave their formal approval. Bonaparte, Siéyès, and Roger-Ducos were appointed provisional Consuls. The clumsy farce was over.

This outcome was not according to the plans of either Siéyès or Napoleon. Both were men of order, and they had expected to overthrow the government in a dignified constitutional manner. The irruption of Murat's grenadiers upset the precarious balance between the civilian element and the military. The Five Hundred had yielded to the force of bayonets: the fact was fraught with consequences. In a triumvirate of equals Siéyès, supported by Roger-Ducos, would have been supreme. But Napoleon, "the God of Fortune and of War", made himself First Consul and grabbed the substance of power. Siéyès was shrewd enough to acknowledge defeat. He and Roger-Ducos gave up their consulships, and were replaced by Cambacérès and Lebrun, both decorative and discreet men. Siéyès was rewarded with a seat in the new Senate and with a handsome estate at Crosne; he was allowed to walk away with whatever cash the Directory had on hand. He resumed his thought-laden silence; but no one was impressed any more. He died in 1836, a fossil long forgotten, eighty-eight years of age.

But what of his cherished constitution? It is usually taken for granted that it disappeared without a trace. It was an intricate mechanism of checks and balances, and its central pivot was the Grand Elector, a functionary with a lavish civil list and no actual power. Napoleon shrugged that conception away: 'Just a hog being fattened!' (Later he revived the title, with his brother Joseph as the hog.) For that bloated shadow, he substituted a reality, himself. In the whole ninety-five articles only two words mattered: Napoleon Bonaparte. Yet his rule was not a pure military despotism; and although he had the constitution ratified by a plebiscite, his ideal was not Caesarism either; for Caesarism is democratic—or demagogic—and Napoleon despised Demos. The Consulate and the Empire remained true to the Siéyès spirit: they were governments by and for the Third Estate, the bourgeoisie. Willynilly, Napoleon, who spurned the Thermidorians, was destined to remain the Sword of Thermidor.

Siéyès and his class provided not only a spirit, but a definite method, and above all a personnel. Siéyès had always wanted a government of "notables" or prominent citizens; and the surest sign of notability is wealth. According to his formula, authority must come from above, confidence from below. So let the taxpayers choose one-tenth of their numbers, thus forming a communal list of notabilities. The next step of the pyramid, one-tenth of the first, will constitute the departmental list; the last step, one-tenth again, the national list. These notables had no power; they were not even consulted;

but it was from them that the government picked all its functionaries at the various levels. The system was altered in 1802, with the creation of so-called "electoral colleges". But the spirit remained the same. Under Napoleon, there were no elections of genuine representatives until the Hundred Days. Louis XVI had been far more liberal in 1788.

Out of the four assemblies then created, the Council of State—an advisory legal body, a panel of experts, and a supreme administrative tribunal—was appointed by the ruler of the nation. The Tribunate, one hundred tongues who could discuss the proposed laws but not pass upon them, and the Legislative Body, three hundred mutes who could vote but not discuss, were at first selected by the Senate, the only institution that had even a semblance of authority. And the Senate was the prolonged shadow of Siéyès and his group. He, with Roger-Ducos, Cambacérès, and Lebrun, picked out the first thirty-one Senators; these selected twenty-nine more; after that the Senate was to be self-recruiting, adding two members every year until the figure of eighty was reached.

The assemblies counted for little; the officials for much. They were recruited from the notables according to the criteria set by Siéyès. Napoleon, at thirty, away from France for the greater part of the preceding three years, would have been unable to improvise a civilian administration : he had to accept it from the hands of experienced men. Gaudin, for instance, who kept the finances of the Consulate and the Empire on a fairly even keel, was a protégé of Siéyès.

On the whole, Siéyès and his friends did their work well. If the grand phantasmagoria of the Empire was also a solid, down-to-earth, efficient régime, it was chiefly because of their appointment of moderate and competent officials. These men ruled more wisely than the generals would have if they had been entrusted with power; or the *émigrés* if they had resumed their ancient privilege of squandering the resources of the state; or the politicians if, directly or indirectly, they had seized control of administrative functions. For a century and a half, France, under a dozen régimes, has remained a bureaucracy with strong traditions and a firm hierarchy. And this solid armature, so necessary in a nation of incurable individualists, assumed its present form on the morrow of Brumaire.

There have been in French history a few miraculous dawns: in 1515, the accession of Francis I, the gay young knight in whom medieval romance blended with the early glow of the Renaissance; in 1661, the assumption of personal power by another young monarch, handsome and eager, Louis XIV. The first two years of the Consulate have the same quality of confident, illimitable hope. Each of these movements might be described as a New Deal: not an upheaval, but a fulfilment of national destiny.

Even the features of the First Consul seemed to respond to the auspicious climate. He was no longer the tense, lean Puss-in-Boots of 1795, pathetic, ludicrous, and disquieting. His face had filled, his complexion had cleared, the daimonic fire had tempered to a glow of quiet authority. For a fleeting hour, at the very summit, he remained human. And Josephine was smiling by his side. He had returned from Egypt determined to discard her. She, aware of the menace, had gone out to meet him, guessed the wrong route, and missed him. So his family caught hold of him first, bitterly unanimous in their denunciations. She forced her way into his house and sobbed all night before an inexorable door. Her children, Eugene and Hortense, joined in her supplications. The door opened: Napoleon had relented. After the storm they were happy. The First Consul was well worth having; but apart from self-interest, Josephine may have been moved by gratitude. And although his passion had abated and his illusions had been dispelled, he still appreciated her charm. She was an admirable hostess. She made old Jacobins and returned *émigrés* feel equally at home. The cynicism of the Barras-Tallien era was frowned upon; decency was the order of the day; soon Talleyrand was compelled to make an honest woman of Mme Grant. But the rigidity of imperial etiquette had not yet set in. There were happy days even in the stately and morose Tuileries, and particularly at La Malmaison, where the hero could still play blindman's buff.

The first acts of Napoleon confirmed the hopes of the people. On December 26, 1799, he wrote open letters to George III and the German Emperor, urging peace. On 7 February, 1800, he declared days of public mourning in honour of George Washington. On 13 February the Bank of France was established. On the 19th the First Consul moved to the Tuileries. On the 20th he spurned an offer from the Bourbon pretender, Louis XVIII, to play the part of a General Monk and, as Constable of France, to become the first subject in a restored monarchy. Every one of these steps endeared him to public opinion: they promised peace and stability, with no return to the old régime.

In the euphoria of this political honeymoon, measures of less favourable omen received little notice. The prefectoral system was created on 17 February, 1800, saddling France with a rigorous centralization that is still a curse. On the same day sixty out of the seventy-three political newspapers were suppressed; more were to follow, and censorship was clamped on the drama as well. French thought was to be absolutely free, provided that the fundamental dogma was not challenged—namely, that France and Napoleon were one, and that dissent was treason. Mme de Staël, who thought for herself and loved to think aloud, was snubbed as a public nuisance until she was exiled as a public enemy.

England and Austria had not responded to Napoleon's advances. Peace had to be won on the battlefield. On 6 May, 1800, Napoleon left for the second Italian campaign. His troops crossed the Alps by way of the Great St. Bernard Pass: guns had to be hauled in hollowed trunks by teams of a hundred men. On 2 June Napoleon entered Milan. On 18 June, not quite according to his plans, he met the Austrians at Marengo.

This time again there was an odd twist to his fate. Napoleon's troops were not routed, but they had decidedly the worst of the encounter. Melas, the Austrian general, had already dispatched news of his victory and turned the pursuit over to a subordinate. Napoleon's lieutenant, Desaix, at the head of a detached corps, rallied to the main body. His forces were exhausted by the march, but their spirit was unbroken. This was best expressed by the famous words: 'The battle is lost: we have time to win another.' A charge led by Kellermann, son of the hero of Valmy, clinched the victory. Desaix died in the hour of triumph.

The battle was not decisive: Melas could have resumed fighting the next day, and Austria refused to make peace. Yet Marengo was hailed at the time as a most brilliant achievement. Perhaps this was due to a feeling of relief. It was a bold gamble for the head of a new government to risk his all on the battlefield. He nearly was defeated; he might have been killed instead of Desaix. Already shrewd speculators like Fouché and Talleyrand had considered the possible emergency. They and their kind were all the louder in their praises of the returning hero. Napoleon was enough of a realist to read their thoughts. He knew that, in order to retain their loyalty, he was doomed to eternal success.

It took the great victory of Moreau at Hohenlinden (3 December, 1800) to break Austria's stubborn pride. On 9 February, 1801, the peace of Lunéville was signed. In October, preliminaries were agreed upon in London; on 25-7 March, 1802, they became the peace of Amiens. Other treaties were negotiated with Russia, Turkey, Prussia, and Bavaria. After ten years of incessant warfare the guns were stilled at last; and in the solemn hush there rose a hymn of gratitude to the genius who had so gloriously closed the tragic era.

Peace abroad, appeasement at home : France should be made livable for all law-abiding Frenchmen. Josephine and Fouché were particularly active in helping returned *émigrés* recover their legal status. Fouché, the regicide and former terrorist, was singularly gentle with them, provided that they did not engage in conspiracies; and the dread Minister of Police became, unexpectedly, a social favourite in the stronghold of the old nobility, the Faubourg Saint-Germain. But he opposed a general amnesty. He found special measures of clemency politically safer and financially more profitable. Talleyrand, who belonged to one of the most ancient and most illustrious families in France, filled his drawing-rooms with members of the aristocracy. Under his courtly and ironical smile, men of proud lineage, bourgeois officials, profiteers, and plebeian generals jostled one another, with a smirk that barely concealed a snarl.

This eclectic policy, this deliberate blending of the *élites,* was intended to hasten the convalescence of French society. Other measures were to serve as the framework of a new France. Napoleon called them "masses of granite". They are even more impressive than his military exploits. The prefectoral system, the Civil Code, the Concordat, the Legion of Honour, the University of France, all had their inception in those two miraculous years, though some of them were not completed until 1807 or 1808. They worked; and they are so convenient to the central power that eight or ten régimes in succession have carefully preserved most of them. Whether they are as beneficial as they are imposing remains a moot question.

In 1799 the civil laws of France were a jungle. Written law in the south, custom law in the north, canon law as a model of procedure, the innumerable edicts and ordinances of the kings, a huge mass of revolutionary legislation, were confusedly struggling for survival. Several proposals had been made to clear up that legal chaos, in particular by Cambacérès (1753-1824). A noted epicure, and a most expert political trimmer, he was also a great jurist, born and bred in the "nobility of the robe". On the morrow of the Brumaire *coup d'état*, commissions were appointed to compile a code. The actual drafting was entrusted to four great lawyers: Tronchet, Portalis, Bigot de Préameneu, Maleville. They completed their work in four months: the project appeared in print on 1 January, 1801. Then it was discussed in general sessions of the Council of State.

In the lull that followed Marengo, Napoleon frequently presided with his usual energy. 'Wake up!' he told his assembly of sedate administrators, nodding at two o'clock in the morning. 'We are here to earn the pay the Republic is giving us.' Had he been an ordinary layman, some of his interventions would have caused a lifting of learned eyebrows: but he was the First Consul and not to be pooh-poohed. His influence, as a rule, was on the conservative side. The amended draft went, section by section ("Title") from the Council of State to the Tribunate and the Legislative Body. Differences were smoothed out in conferences presided over by Cambacérès. The Civil Code became law on 21 March, 1804.

Three years later it was renamed *Code Napoléon,* and to this day the orthodox believe that it sprang verbatim from the hero's omniscience. It survived, not only in France, but in parts of western Germany; and it was adopted by the state of Louisiana. It confirmed the essential doctrine of the Enlightenment and of the early Revolution: the abolition of privileges, the equality of all French *men* before the law (women were kept in subjection). It also embodied the Thermidorian principle: the sovereign rights of the propertied classes. This was most tersely expressed in Article 1781, which it took sixty years to expunge: "The master's word is taken: as to the rate of wages; the payment of the salary of the previous year; and the advances on the salary of the current year." No civil equality between masters and men.

Nothing is more Napoleonic than the Concordat with the Pope: a swift and dazzling victory, swiftly followed by an irremediable breach, and a full century of bickerings. To clear away inveterate misconceptions, a fact and a few words should be borne in mind. The fact: within six years the Pope was a prisoner, and the Emperor excommunicated. The words—Napoleon's own: "The Concordat was my worst mistake."

The spasmodic attempts of fanatical minorities to root out the Christian faith had ended in 1794. The cult of Reason had been a brief local show; that of the Supreme Being, a form of "natural religion", had died with Robespierre. On 18 September, 1794, all connections had been severed between Church and State. Under the Directory, Catholic worship was free; the Constitutional Church survived, somewhat languidly; Protestantism had at last a full chance; and new religious bodies appeared, such as the Theophilanthropists.

This régime of liberty was anathema to Napoleon's love of unity and discipline. He might have borrowed the ancient motto: *"Une foi, une loi, un roi"*, one faith, one law, one king, a curious anticipation of Nazi totalitarianism. He had excellent reasons for seeking an alliance with the Church. There was a strong reaction against the rationalism of Voltaire and Diderot. The sentimental, aesthetic, romantic return to religion, heralded by Rousseau, was to find its gospel in Chateaubriand's *Génie du Christianisme*.[1] The strongest argument, in Napoleon's own mind, was that society could not exist without economic and social inequality: religion alone could make that harsh reality acceptable to the masses. *"Il faute une religion pour le peuple"* (the common folk must have a religion) was a corollary of the Thermidorian belief in wealth. But the Thermidorians found an obstacle on their path to Rome: they had bought Church property at bargain prices, and the Church had never accepted the loss.

Pius VII, shrewd as well as meek, was ready for an understanding. His States were at the mercy of the French armies. He hated that arch-heresy, the separation of Church and State. He desired to end the constitutional schism, which refused to die of its own accord, and was a menace as well as a scandal. The prestige of the Holy See would be greatly enhanced if victorious France officially returned to the fold. And he saw the possibility of assuming over the French clergy a direct authority in matters of discipline which his predecessors had never possessed.

The negotiations were long and tangled. They resulted in the Concordat of 15 July, 1801. But the spirit

[1] Published 14 April, 1802; fragments had appeared earlier.

of the Enlightenment was still strong among the bourgeoisie, who were the mainstay of the régime: it was only
on 8 April, 1802, that the Concordat could be promulgated
as a law. Ten days later, on Easter Sunday, a solemn *Te
Deum* at Notre-Dame returned thanks for the restoration
of a religious peace. The schism was ended; the Catholic
Church was officially recognized; the clergy were to
receive salaries from the State; the Pope and the temporal
ruler of France would in unison appoint the bishops; the
purchasers of Church property would be left undisturbed.
Napoleon had wrested from the royalists their strongest
asset: the support of Rome. Henceforth he could boast of
'My Prefects, my Bishops, my police. . . .'

Hardly had the incense of the *Te Deum* dis-
persed when the irremediable conflict surged up again.
Napoleon was incapable of sharing power. To his mind,
"the things that are Caesar's" embraced all earthly things,
particularly Church property and Church discipline. It
was an ancient conflict, as ancient as Constantine: if
associated, the temporal and the spiritual must fight for
supremacy. The quarrel had torn medieval Germany,
and the Emperor had to go to Canossa. But a French
king had humbled the Papacy in 1303, and under Louis
XIV Bossuet had drawn up the charter of Gallicanism:
while remaining in spiritual communion with Rome, the
French Church claimed the right to administer herself
freely, under the protection of the anointed king. In the
Pope's mind, the Concordat was to mark the triumph
of ultramontanism, the Pontiff sole and absolute ruler of
the Church throughout the world. In Napoleon's, it meant
the confirmation of Gallicanism: the supremacy of the
national sovereign even in the ecclesiastical domain. On
his own authority, and without consulting the Pope,
Napoleon added to the Concordat "Organic Articles" that
boldly reaffirmed Bossuet's position. The Concordat, a

disingenuous compromise, hampered the life of the Church for a hundred years, without strengthening the State. When it was denounced at last, the result was two-fold: a great spiritual awakening among the Catholics and the waning of anti-clericalism. The Concordat appeared as a brilliant tactical victory, but victory never is a substitute for wisdom.

Destiny, the coincidence of luck and genius, had served Napoleon marvellously well: in 1802 he was without question "first in war, first in peace, first in the hearts of his countrymen". Mme Letizia is reputed to have said: *'Pourvu que cela dure!'* (If only it would last!) It did not last: by the end of 1802, the honeymoon of France and the young hero was already over. What is to follow is an entrancing drama, but no longer solid reality; a titanic quest for the unattainable, a gorgeous and feverish dream.

CHAPTER FOUR

THE PARTING OF THE WAYS

NAPOLEON BONAPARTE: CONSUL FOR LIFE

1802—1804

ON 1 August, 1802, Napoleon, at his urgent request, was proclaimed Consul for Life. His next birthday, on the 15th, was celebrated with elaborate rejoicings: a new glory was thus imparted to the Feast of the Assumption. The amended constitution was ratified by the usual perfunctory and slipshod plebiscite: out of a population of thirty million, three million expressed approval. The vote was taken on open registers; in the villages, there were long lists of names written in the same hand.

The discrepancy between labels and realities, of which we could quote many instances, is particularly striking in the case of the Consulate. The decisive change came, not in 1799 and not in 1804, but in 1802. The consulship for ten years entrusted to Citizen Bonaparte was still, and might have remained, a republican function. When in 1802 Napoleon Bonaparte, for thus he now styled himself, became Consul for Life, with the right of choosing his successor, the Empire was made. Its formal proclamation two years later simply involved stiffer and gaudier trappings. In 1802 a few men, of very different statures, realized the gravity of the change. One of them was Lazare Carnot, the Organizer of Victory; another was the enigmatic Fouché. They understood the principle at stake: it was indeed the point of no return. But for most of the contemporaries, and for most historians as well, 1802 was only a minor step. Power remained in the same hands, under the same institutions. True enough: but the power had changed its nature, and the institutions had become shadows.

From 1789 to 1799 the destiny of France and that of Napoleon had been converging. In 1799 they met and merged. For over two years it seemed as though the nation and the young leader were miraculously one. In 1802 their paths diverged. This moment marks the beginning of the purely Napoleonic saga, dazzling, tragic, and unreal. France was committed to the formidable adventure: not of her own volition, but because of bit, bridle, and spur.

When opinion has no free outlet, conspiracies become the only hope. A desperate remedy, for at that time every conspiracy contained the threat of civil war, with foreign powers intervening. The desire for rebellion was not unanimous, even when the disenchantment had followed the glorious dawn of the Consulate. In 1802-4 Napoleon was not loved—he never was loved until after his death, and then only *against* his victors. But he was not purely and simply feared. His could be called a government by consent, if consent be equated with resignation. He was accepted by most Frenchmen, not as a positive good, but as the least of several assorted evils. The heirs of the Revolution saw in him a shield against a return to the old régime—an old régime aggravated by the bitterness of revenge. For the profiteers of the Revolution, the Thermidorians, he was a shield against social democracy.

For all Frenchmen, he was a shield against foreign invasion.

The chief danger to his rule came, not from the Jacobins, but from the royalists. Robespierre and his closest associates had been destroyed in Thermidor (1794). The last Montagnards, defeated in Prairial (20 May, 1795), had stabbed themselves to death, passing the dagger from hand to hand. On 24 December, 1800, as the First Consul was going to the opera through the narrow rue Saint-Nicaise, a bomb or "infernal machine" was hurled at his carriage. There were many victims; he went unscathed. He at once affected to believe, because he wanted to believe, that the "anarchists", heirs of the Terrorists, were responsible for the outrage. It suited his book: he was attempting to rally the moderate elements to his cause, or rather to his person, and the red bogy had been effective on the 18th Brumaire. So one hundred and thirty "extremists" were deported on general suspicion. Later it was discovered that the culprits were royalists: two of them, mere instruments, were duly executed on 26 April, 1801. But Napoleon thought it best to keep the radicals out of harm's way; and they were left to rot alive in Guiana.

Out of that complicated series of intrigues—"tenebrous affairs", to use Balzac's words—three names emerge, and three men may serve as symbols: Cadoudal, Moreau, and the Duke of Enghien. Georges Cadoudal was a fit hero for an Alexandre Dumas romance. From the very first, in 1793, he had fought in the west against the Revolution. Captured, he escaped and fought again. When organized resistance collapsed, he resorted to plotting: he had a hand in the rue Saint-Nicaise affair. Napoleon respected a man as determined and as ruthless as himself: in 1800, he granted him an interview. After all, the new régime and the royalists were fellow travellers. But Georges was a man of faith and could not be snared. He fled to England and returned secretly, in 1803, with British gold. The plot involved the assassination of the First Consul, an insurrection in Paris, and—the ever-frustrated dream of the royalists—the presence of a royal prince. Cadoudal was thwarted, but for several months he managed to elude the police. He was arrested in March 1804. A plea received from Josephine obtained a reprieve for those of his accomplices who were of noble birth; Cadoudal, a commoner, was executed on 4 June, 1804. He could then remark with a bitter smile: 'We have worked better than we knew; instead of a king, we are giving France an emperor.'

The Moreau affair is more ambiguous. Moreau was the only military man whose fame could balance that of Bonaparte: Hohenlinden had been a more brilliant victory than Marengo. If Cadoudal was openly a royalist, Moreau was no less decidedly a republican. His wife, a Creole like Josephine, spurred his political ambitions; not very successfully, for Moreau was exceedingly cautious and was at his best in a masterly retreat. He disapproved, and not simply out of jealousy, of Napoleon's rise to absolute power. He certainly was approached by Cadoudal: how he responded remains doubtful. Napoleon had him arrested and was hoping for a death sentence; by commuting it, he would reduce his one great rival to impotence. But Moreau was acquitted. At a second trial, under extreme pressure, the court brought out an equivocal verdict, with a penalty of two years' imprisonment. Moreau in jail would have been a greater threat than ever: Napoleon made him accept banishment to America instead, with a profitable liquidation of his estate in France.

Most mysterious of all is the case of the Duke of

Enghien. The facts are plain enough; their motivation still eludes us. A spy revealed that a young prince, a scion of the great Bourbon-Condé family, was living at Ettenheim in Baden. Napoleon must have come to the conclusion that he was the one the royalists expected to appear when the Cadoudal conspiracy matured. He sent Caulaincourt, a general and diplomat of aristocratic birth, to arrest him. It was not Caulaincourt, but his subordinate Ordener who actually captured the victim. But his half-blind and reluctant participation in that high-handed affair darkened the career and preyed upon the mind of Caulaincourt, an attractive figure in an epoch not notable for chivalric virtues. Enghien was taken to the castle of Vincennes, near Paris; judged by a drumhead court martial, he was shot at half-past two the next morning.

Napoleon himself denied that he had intended to send a last-minute reprieve : he would not indulge in a bit of melodrama like the one that spared Dostoievski's life. He accepted full responsibility for the deed: were not the Bourbons keeping sixty would-be assassins in Paris? In fact, the breach of international law and the secret trial were mere peccadilloes in Napoleon's heavy record. Although Enghien was quiescent at the time, he was Napoleon's declared enemy, lived a few miles from the frontier, and was supported by English subsidies. It was not so much a crime as an error. Enghien simply was the wrong man. The error, however, turned into a blunder of the first magnitude. For the death of Enghien roused feelings of profound horror among those who believed in the sacred virtue of princely blood. It caused Chateaubriand to quit the service of Napoleon and gradually to turn into his implacable enemy. Incidentally, the famous phrase: "Worse than a crime: a blunder", so perfectly in the style of Talleyrand or Fouché probably belongs to the very able but dimly remembered Boulay de la Meurthe.

Napoleon was not incapable of capricious and ruthless action. He gambled on intuitions, which in many cases led him to triumph. But, although not shirking his responsibility in this tragic affair, he repeatedly and publicly accused Talleyrand of having advised the step. Certain it is that Talleyrand was fully aware of the facts. He was present, with Cambacérès and Lebrun, when the decision was taken; and it was he who gave Caulaincourt his instructions. Whether he originated the whole scheme is a different problem. On the basis of available documents that problem is insoluble. Talleyrand did not deny Napoleon's point-blank accusations; but he could not have done so without exposing his life. Later, he deliberately destroyed every particle of evidence in the government's archives which might prove embarrassing to him; and his *Memoirs* are a vast quagmire of evasions and deceptions. Had Fouché been Napoleon's evil counsellor in this case, the situation would be clear. Fouché, a regicide and a Terrorist, would obviously want to create a gulf between the First Consul and the royalists. But Fouché's influence was not predominant at the time. He was glad to let others—Murat, Savary, Hulin—do the dirty work while he rubbed his hands and smiled his bland and furtive smile.

This obscure affair evokes a wider and still more baffling mystery: the relations between Napoleon and Talleyrand. For seventeen years they were compounded of fascination and hatred, of mutual appreciation and mutual contempt. Talleyrand, as early as 1797, saw in Bonaparte the coming man and attached himself to his fortune. He was also among the first to discover that the Master was not "civilized", as he put it, not ruled by common sense and a realistic view of the possible. By 1807, he was positive that Napoleon was no longer sane. While still a great dignitary of the Empire, he plainly told Alexander of Russia that in the interest of France and of Europe the madman should be destroyed. Napoleon, who prided himself on his knowledge of men, was not fully aware until 1814 of Talleyrand's implacable enmity.

He suspected him, and could not bring himself to discard him. Why? He was no doubt impressed by the great name of Talleyrand-Périgord. What a triumph for the penurious petty "nobleman" from wild Corsica to be served by a man whose ancestor, eight hundred years before, had asked Hugh Capet: "Who made thee king?" He who had been dazzled by the meretricious graces of Thermidorian society was awed by the pure *ancien régime* quality of Talleyrand's *savoir-vivre*, his lavish luxury that never smacked of the parvenu, his cool ironic superiority veiled but enhanced through his exquisite courtesy. Before Talleyrand, Napoleon felt uncouth. He hated him for it, as Nero hated Petronius Arbiter. But he never dared to crush him, for fear that the victim's last smile would mean: "What else could you expect of such a vulgarian?" He knew that Talleyrand was corrupt to the core; that, in any diplomatic negotiation, his first broad hint was: 'How much for me?'; that he was an expert at procuring women for himself and for others, including Napoleon. But Napoleon's Swiftian misanthropy was baffled and fascinated by a depravity so much richer than his own. Somehow Talleyrand's impeccable courtliness brought out the foul-mouthed trooper in Napoleon. The Emperor publicly called his former Minister of Foreign Affairs, Prince of Benevento, Vice-Grand Elector of the Empire: *'De la merde dans un bas de soie!'* (s—t in a silk stocking). But as he strode

furiously away, he must have read in advance on
Talleyrand's imperturbable face the avenging words:
'What a pity that such a great man should be so
ill-bred!'

As there is a Napoleonic legend, so there is a Talleyrand legend, hardly less indestructible. To the fairy tale
of Napoleon's invincibility (remember that he lost six
campaigns out of twelve), corresponds the inveterate
tradition of Talleyrand's infallible sagacity. It would be
instructive to list the major blunders of that supreme
statesman and diplomat. His grand manner still impresses
modern historians; his unadulterated corruption seems to
them the very perfection of "realism". At any rate, he was
free from the "virtue" that made Robespierre an abomina-
tion, and from the "chivalry" that made Lafayette a
laughing-stock.

Cadoudal's complex conspiracies came to light, even
though the light has a dubious quality. A few others,
without attracting public attention, were fairly well
known: in particular the first attempt of General Malet
in 1808. But more important than the definite episodes
is the secret history—the underground discontent, the
quiet preventive measures, the thwarted plots. If on
the surface the course of the Empire was untroubled at
home, it was because Fouché was in power again from
1804 to 1810, and because, even after his dismissal, the
redoubtable machine he had created still functioned,
even in the clumsy hands of a Savary. Fouché was more
than a chief of police: he had the prefects report directly
to him, and this made him in fact a Minister of the
Interior. Siéyès had dreamed of a republic with two consuls, one for war, the other for peace. This conception,
though unacknowledged, prevailed almost literally under

the Empire: Napoleon fighting the foreign enemy, Fouché repressing disorder at home. Wherever two or three were gathered together, one at least was Fouché's agent; at any rate, he deliberately fostered that legend.

By definition, the arch-policeman should be the arch-villain: sinister of countenance, exuding cruelty and corruption out of every pore. Fouché was not prepossessing, but he was colourless rather than hideous. He was too clever a man to flaunt his iniquities; and in social relations he was curiously affable. His private life was happy and pure, almost a miracle in those days. He had principles: they happened to coincide with his interests, but that made them all the firmer. He remained loyal to the spirit of the Revolution, and he supported the Empire—not necessarily the Emperor—as long as the new régime remained true to its origins. He amassed a modest fortune—some thirteen million francs at a time when the franc went much farther than the dollar does today.[1] Considering his opportunities—control of the underworld and judicious favours payable both in gratitude and in cash—he showed more discretion than many an army contractor or marshal. Talleyrand made forty million out of diplomacy: the reorganization of Germany in 1803 and the Congress of Vienna were gold mines to him. Napoleon himself could boast that his purely private hoard amounted to more than two hundred million. Even graft in those epic days was on a monumental scale: loot to match the Arc de Triomphe.

The peace of Amiens had been hailed with joy on both sides of the Channel; perhaps with even greater

---

1 3fr. 35 was a fair day's wage for a skilled worker.

relief in London than in Paris. In spite of three different Hundred Years wars—or because of them—the two countries are linked by an ambivalent and undeniable mutual fascination: Anglomania and Anglophobia are both perennial in France, and so are their British equivalents in England. As soon as the treaty was signed, tourists by the thousands rushed to the Continent. The peace was reasonable—not dictated, not vindictive, it respected the vital interests of both parties. Yet it lasted only fourteen months.

French public opinion at the time, and for generations thereafter, made "perfidious Albion" responsible for the breach; and the wilful lack of logic in British policy may easily appear as deviousness. England, of course, put all the blame on Napoleon's insensate and brutal aggressiveness.

After one hundred and fifty years, research has not yet built up an irrefutable case for either side. The key to that problem is the central point in our study: the personality of Napoleon. Here history and biography are one.

As for England's irreconcilable opposition, the facts refuse to bow before the theories of historians. In 1802 England freely acknowledged the new boundaries of France. She had not been cudgelled into sullen acquiescence. She did not resent Amiens as a shameful peace. She received the news with almost unanimous joy. France held Antwerp for twenty years; and that "pistol levelled at the heart of England" never was a serious menace. The peril came from Boulogne. For centuries before Amiens, for a century and a half after Amiens, England accepted French rule over the vital Channel ports.

I firmly believe that it was as unnecessary as it was disastrous for England to join in 1793 the coalition against France. She should have preserved a friendly neutrality: Priestley was right and Burke was wrong. The Revolution stood closer to English principles than did the Continental autocracies; and England too had beheaded a king. With England's friendly support, the Republic might have remained liberal, perhaps under a Danton. It was England's unreasoning enmity that prepared the way for Napoleon. But in 1803 Napoleon was a fact. The peace of Amiens became a scrap of paper, because it failed to curb the conqueror's enormous greed. For he was not satisfied with the "natural frontiers": he must keep control of Italy, of western Germany. "And tomorrow the world": Spain, Holland, and their far-flung empires; Constantinople, India; even North America, for the transfer of Louisiana back from Spain to France and the Haiti expedition were manifest signs.

I am therefore inclined to minimize the responsibility of England in the resumption of hostilities. More paradoxically, I am inclined also to reduce her share in the final victory. Thanks to her impregnability and to her wealth, England provided a constant centre of opposition; but she could not deliver the knock-out blow. If, supreme on land, Napoleon finally collapsed, it was not through Mahan's "influence of sea power", but because he was unable to treat the conquered and the neutrals as his friends and allies. Their pride and interests counted for nothing; his will, and his will alone, was law; and that will was boundless. That is to say, it was mad. But for Napoleon's incurable *Napoleonism*, Trafalgar need not have proved decisive, and the Continental Blockade might have been successful.

There is in French folklore a character, Joseph Prud-homme, who has the gift of exaggerating truisms into absurdities. He said: 'If Napoleon had remained a lieutenant of artillery, he would not have fallen from his throne'. Marshal Foch rose to the same height: 'Napoleon was truly great: what a pity that he was so ambitious!' What the comic character and the great warrior failed to acknowledge is that, with Napoleon, *greatness* and *ambition* were identical. Ambition with him was that flaw—it may be an excess of virtue—which, according to Aristotle, drives the tragic hero into the abyss of his fate, but also marks him as a hero.

Napoleon's ambition is unique because of its absolute purity. It was not bound by paltry aims. He had ambition, not ambitions. He rightly said: 'I am not ambitious: at any rate, my ambition is so intimately bound up with my whole being that it cannot be distinguished from it.' Other great leaders have identified their personality and their cause—Mohammed, Rousseau, Hitler, Franklin Roosevelt, Charles de Gaulle. It is the messianic complex: "I, and I alone, am the Way." Still, in all these cases, there was a faith, there was a cause. Napoleon's creed is summed up in one commandment: "Thou shalt have no other god beside Napoleon." In him, personality was more than egotism, more even than egomania; it reached the level of solipsism: in his eyes, he alone existed. He might have taken as his motto the words of his favourite poet, Corneille: *"Moi seul, et c'est assez"* (I, myself, alone, and that suffices). A city welcomed him with a streamer, blasphemous and profoundly true: *"Sum qui sum"* (I am that I am). This was felt from the first by people who knew him well, admired him freely, but refused to fall down and worship him: his brother Lucien as early as 1792, Mme de Staël in 1797: 'For him, there is only one person, himself; all others are ciphers.' This raises him immensely above the *prima donna* who merely seeks applause: he felt the same contempt for praise as for blame.

This formidable hypertrophy of the ego—one of the essential traits of romanticism—was not created, but made possible by historical circumstances. He was so situated that there was no cause available for him to serve except his own. Not patriotism: the famous phrase: "I wish to repose on the banks of the Seine, among those French people I have loved so well," is outrageous propaganda. He was a Corsican patriot, and he hated the French: his little country disappeared as a political entity, and France became his instrument, but he never became a Frenchman at heart. He was not even a European: he would gladly have become a sultan, a rajah, best of all a Grand Mogul. He was attached to no class: by thin courtesy a patrician, he had no traditions in common with the French aristocracy; he hated the rabble, he despised the bourgeoisie. Even the army was not his family. For only a few of his generals—Lannes, Duroc, Junot—did he feel any genuine friendship. He loved his soldiers as his tools, not as his comrades. In Spain, when, ready to mutiny, they cried: 'He treats us like convicts! Damn him! Shoot him!' He whipped them into submission: 'Oh! You want to go back to Paris and enjoy yourselves! I mean to keep you with the colours until you are eighty!' To Metternich he said: 'A man like me does not care a damn for a million lives.'

He had no faith in human nature. He had seen the frivolity of the aristocrats, the shameful cowardice of the King, the ferocity of the mob, the brutality of the soldiers, the corruption of the profiteers; even love had come to him through a woman whom he could not respect. He had no philosophy: in his youth he had been devoted to Rousseau, and later he appreciated the acid common sense of Voltaire; but he came to despise all thought as "ideology", to consider thought as his personal enemy; and rightly so, for thought is freedom. He had no religion. He was ready to use any faith—Islam or Catholicism— for political purposes, or as "an opiate for the people". He professed at times a very commonplace theism; but, more definitely, the coarsest materialism : life is nothing but physics and chemistry. Beyond his reach—for he was great enough to look beyond—he acknowledged, not a Power that makes for righteousness, but only blind Fate. When you tear off the trappings of soldier and ruler, you find, not a frightened and shrivelled creature, not even a perverted soul, but a mystery, impenetrable because it is a vacuum. Napoleon is nothing but Napoleon.

Honours and wealth : these he grabbed as he went, roughly, abundantly, contemptuously, for his aim was beyond them. It was even beyond power : power was but his instrument, "his violin", as he put it. His sole aim was *glory:* again a word he may have learned from Corneille; and thirst for glory is another phrase for ego-worship. His monuments of bronze or stone are altars to glory—his own; and his institutions, his Legion of Honour, his Code, were turned into so many Arches of Triumph.

The very nature of such a thirst for glory is to be unquenchable. The morrow of every victory is an anti-climax : there must ever be new prodigies, each more dazzling than the last. He was the eternal Don Juan of politics and war. He put it himself with daring and forcible humour : 'God the Father's job? Not for me; no future to it; a blind alley.'[1]

1 Lessing had said something of the kind: the truth in the making is greater than the truth absolute; and Balzac, most Napoleonic of romancers, shows in *Melmoth Reconciled* the infinite weariness of omnipotence attained.

Hence also his wild gambling with fate. It was not in his nature to cash his chips and retire. To rest satisfied, to calculate on safe and modest profits, would seem to him craven and commonplace: the true hero stakes his all—world empire or downfall. So nothing with him could ever be final: material success, power, victory, were but stepping-stones to higher things. A power that is not boundless, that can be checked by a constitution or a treaty, seemed to him no power at all. This can be translated into very concrete terms. He was glad to sign the peace of Amiens because, as he saw it, it would open, not close, his way to further conquest. When the British reminded him that it was a curb, he accused them of wanting his destruction. A reasonable understanding with Alexander in 1812, a compromise with the Allies in 1813, would have been in his eyes stale and unprofitable. His destiny was the breathless unceasing course. Whosoever wanted him to stop, even though it were to rest in triumph, was his declared enemy.

Paradoxically, he faced without flinching, he almost welcomed, the idea of defeat. Better an epic defeat than a tame victory. The greatest heroes of mankind, in thought or arms, in fact or fable, have met disastrous ends: Prometheus, Socrates, Caesar, Jesus, Roland. There is no triumph so pure and so lasting as martyrdom. On the epic plane he had chosen, Napoleon was right. There is no comparison between the hold he still has on our imagination, and the sober tributes we pay to Frederick the Great, Washington, Wellington, Bismarck. Had he played his cards more shrewdly, he would have won an honoured place in history, but he would not be a demi-god. The saga needed the *Götterdämmerung*, Moscow aflame, the Berezina choked with icefloes and corpses, Leipzig and the Battle of the Nations, the farewell to the Old Guard at Fontainebleau, Waterloo, St. Helena.

If Napoleon were but the martinet, the unscrupulous politician, the efficiency expert, the short and pudgy central figure in a stiff pageant, and, from beginning to end, the Sword of Thermidor, an indelible stain of vulgarity would cling to his fame. He was all that, and the vulgarity is there: but his heroic and lucid madness redeems and transmutes that thick worldly success. It lifts him, as he knew and desired, among the great myths of mankind, Alexander, Caesar, Charlemagne; and more definitely, among the great romantic myths, his contemporaries: Prometheus, Faust, Don Juan. This place he coveted, strove for, conquered; and it cannot be taken away from him.

Mental asylums are filled with world conquerors. The cream of the jest is that Napoleon, too, laboured under the delusion that he was Napoleon—and lo! he *was* Napoleon. For his crazy dream was served by such marvellous luck and such matchless efficiency, it had captured such an array of enormous forces, that even today it wins at least our willing suspension of disbelief. It has the degree of realism which marks the supreme fairy tales. It is too vivid and too consistent not to be, at least in the aesthetic realm, almost as good as true. After one hundred and fifty years we still love to imagine that but for an unkind trick of fate it might have become sober truth.

The career of Napoleon after 1802 is no longer hemmed in by factual history; it is poetry, a triumph of the imagination. It tallies perfectly with Kant's definition of art: *Zweckmässigkeit ohne Zweck,* adequacy to purpose without purpose, or, more tersely, art for art's sake. To count the cost would be sheer Philistinism. Who cares about the death of one million vague human beings?

The gesture was beautiful. The dead are dead: the glory is alive. And Americans, the most practical of men and also the most romantic, still flock reverently to His tomb.

CHAPTER FIVE

NAPOLEON EMPEROR

THE ASCENDING STAR

1804—1807

On 18 May, 1804, the Senate proclaimed Napoleon Emperor of the French. Lazare Carnot had protested again, in a noble and hopeless speech. This time Fouché was not on the same side. On the contrary, it was he who had steered the Senate to meet the desire of the Master; and he was rewarded with his favourite post, the Ministry of Police. As an old Jacobin, Fouché was reassured by the sacrifice of the Duke of Enghien: it looked as though Napoleon, Emperor of the Republic, had committed himself to the cause of the Revolution.

For the third time, there was a plebiscite: Rousseauistic democracy—the Will of the People, the Social Contract—was given this Platonic satisfaction. The result was impressive: again three million and a half ayes, in a country of some thirty million, with a pitiful scattering of noes. It was also unconvincing. Louis Madelin, a staunch Napoleonist, gloats over this quasi-unanimity. But he also notes that during that very spring, Parisian opinion had been very restive; that the bar and the bench as well as many elements in the army had openly resented Napoleon's treatment of Moreau; and that, on the proclamation of the Empire, there was a sharp drop in government bonds. Only *sixty-six* people in Paris dared to register dissent; which proves that the plebiscite was either a miracle or a farce.

The Empire was declared hereditary; but the line of descent was not clearly defined. This greatly chagrined Joseph, who, as the eldest of the clan, believed in his own divine right, and who was encouraged by a small clique to think that he might be a more liberal ruler than his brother. All the Bonapartes, and particularly the great man's sisters, scrambled wildly for honours and prerogatives, 'As if,' Napoleon sardonically remarked, 'they were fighting over the heritage of our father the king'. Only three kept, or were kept aloof: Mme Letizia, still shrugging her shoulders, unconvinced that 'there ever was such an empire'; Lucien and Jerome, who had contracted unsuitable marriages. Jerome came to heel and gave up his American wife, Elizabeth Patterson. Lucien stood firm and remained in opposition until the Hundred Days.

All the Bonapartes were one in their hatred of the Beauharnais. The danger of their being passed over was very real. Napoleon was sincerely fond of Eugene: not a commanding personality, but loyal, talented, and above all tractable. Napoleon thought of adopting as his heir the son of his brother Louis and of his stepdaughter Hortense. It was Louis himself who rejected the plan with horror. He affected to believe in the atrocious scandal that the boy was actually Napoleon's son, and that Josephine had connived in the infamous scheme. So Napoleon's heir remained a shadow. It was this ambiguous situation that led, after six years of bitter feuding, to the divorce and the second marriage of Napoleon.

Although the word *Republic* survived for a while, and republican principles were still professed, republican

simplicity was at once discarded for the gorgeousness
of a brand-new régime. Grand dignitaries were created,
with titles of Byzantine splendour. Joseph became Grand
Elector; Cambacérès, Arch Chancellor of the Empire;
Lebrun, Arch Treasurer; Eugene, Arch Chancellor of
State; Louis, Grand Constable; Murat, the dashing
cavalier, Grand Admiral; Duroc, a personal favourite,
sincerely devoted to Napoleon, Grand Marshal of the
Palace; Caulaincourt, Grand Equerry or Master of the
Horse. Sixteen generals were promoted to marshals. Four
years later most of them, and a few civil servants, had
dukedoms conferred upon them.

All this, according to Napoleon, was part of the
"system": to impress Europe, to dazzle France, to reward
the loyal, to bridle the hesitant, to spur the ambitious.
And also to temper or dilute the pretensions of the old
nobility, which, in a thin but steady stream, was rallying
to the new sovereign. He welcomed the aristocrats of the
ancient régime—'Only those people make good servants!'
—but he did not want them to swamp his court.

Princes of the Blood, dignitaries, marshals, had been
made rich by the Master's bounty and were allowed to
grow still richer. But that also was part of the "system":
they were expected to spend their new wealth like the
grands seigneurs of the old school. Mme Letizia refused
to play the game: Josephine played it only too well.
Titles and trappings, the improvised court had all the
glitter of a Shriners' convention. But not the uproarious
good humour. In spite of Josephine's graciousness—the
whilom cocotte had turned into a perfect Empress,
dignified and charming—life at the Tuileries was stiff and
frigid. "Fossils" and "upstarts" were never full reconciled.
Everyone sneered at every glittering title—except his
own: for Cambacérès took himself seriously as a Serene
Highness, addressed by His Majesty as "my cousin", and

even Fouché rather fancied himself as Duke of Otranto. 'There is only one person more absurd than Monsieur Maret: it is the Duke of Bassano': Talleyrand alone could raise his eyebrows impartially at them all—even at the imperial crown.

Louis XIV had been the perfect host: the new Master was curt as a rule, and often rude. He treated women with glaring discourtesy. He inspected them with the baleful glare of a sergeant-major, and publicly criticized their looks, their dresses, their morals. His state dinners were notorious. He might keep the company waiting for hours, and when he rushed in, he bolted his food in twenty minutes. Cambacérès the epicure could afford to smile: he had amply fortified himself beforehand.

Napoleon showed the same imperial egotism in his brief encounters. He had Mlle Duchesnois, a great actress, summoned to the palace; through his valet, he ordered her to undress; he forgot her for loftier concerns; and when reminded of her presence, he sent word for her to dress again.

Yet he could charm when he chose; not merely with the condescension of omnipotence, which delights only the snobs, but with the display of his vivid personality. He won many of his *grognards* with a few words of bluff comradeship (but they kept grumbling all the same). Pope Pius VII, through the bitter storms of their later relations, could never forget the enchantment of their first meeting. Czar Alexander, unsteady, but intelligent and sensitive, was completely won over. And when the Emperor of the West met the High Priest of Western Culture, Goethe, each summed up his impression of the other in the same word: 'Here is a man.' In this, the great play-actor was not a histrion: for the part he played so well was Napoleon.

.   .   .   .   .

The word *Empire* stood for many confused traditions and aspirations: vast dominion, military rule, supremacy. In assuming the imperial title, Napoleon was swimming with a strong if turbid tide. Public opinion accepted the change, if not with exultation, at any rate without demur. Few were the men like Rouget de Lisle (author of the *Marseillaise*), Paul-Louis Courier, Beyle (Stendhal), and Beethoven, who admired the republican leader and felt that when he reached for a crown, he was degrading himself: "He aspires to descend."

Of all the vast shadows evoked by the magic word *Empire*, the most substantial was that of Charlemagne. It was Charlemagne rather than Caesar or Augustus whom Napoleon had before his eyes as a pattern and exemplar. He spoke with deep conviction when he referred to Charlemagne as Emperor of the French, and "our illustrious predecessor". It was the Carolingian precedent that made him desire to be consecrated by the Pope. In the case of Charlemagne himself, and of the German emperors until Frederick III (1440), that ceremony had taken place in Rome. Napoleon, more imperious, summoned the Vicar of Christ to his own capital, as if the Pontiff were his chaplain. The request was unheard of; the Roman Curia, extremely conservative, and violently hostile to a régime of revolutionary origin, considered it as preposterous. Pius VII decided to comply. No doubt he felt the pressure of French power on the frontiers of his States, and he was dazzled by the fabulous prestige of the new master; but his acceptance was dictated by less worldly considerations. In his eyes, the Concordat was still a miracle, and he thought no reward too high for the "man of God" who had accomplished it.

From the personal point of view, the voyage amply fulfilled the Pontiffs' expectations. He was received with veneration throughout that France which he had believed lost to Christianity; Paris, the capital of Voltairian free-thought, was at his feet; the Emperor himself treated him with a unique blend of profound respect and filial affection. The four months of his sojourn were a delight; he returned to Rome laden with costly gifts and still glowing with his triumph, which for him meant the triumph of the faith. On a different plane, however, he came back with empty hands. He had not secured the return of the Legations (Bologna, Ferrara, the Romagna) to the Papal States. Catholicism had not been proclaimed, as he had hoped, the sole official religion of France. The divorce law remained on the statute book. The Gallican virus had not been eliminated from the Organic Articles. In the contest of wits between the two Italians, the *condottiere* had been sharper than the Holy Father.

Another disappointment: the Pope was not allowed to *crown* the Emperor. Napoleon was convinced that he ruled by the direct grace of God and the will of the people. The Church could anoint, consecrate, confirm him: but not assert any authority over him. Power unlimited was the first among "the things which are Caesar's". Ultimately he was to chafe under the distinction between the spiritual and the temporal: "They—the priests—want the nobler part of man, leaving me nought but the carcass." He was beginning to feel himself the Vicar of God: the Pope was but his Imperial Minister of Public Worship, to be dismissed if need be like a Fouché or a Talleyrand. For every totalitarianism is theocracy, and the Napoleonic state was totalitarianism in absolute purity.

The eve of the coronation was marked by a scene of high comedy. Cunningly, Josephine confessed to the Pope that their marriage had been a purely civil one. Pius VII insisted on a religious ceremony. It was performed in haste and secrecy by Uncle Cardinal Fesch, with Berthier,

Duroc, and Talleyrand as the sole witnesses. Napoleon, at the time, was not determined upon divorce; but the thought had crossed his mind, and he did not relish having another obstacle placed in his path. As the solemn historian Albert Sorel puts it, "the vigil of the new Charlemagne was enlivened by a shotgun marriage".

On the morrow, 2 December, 1804, the long ceremony at Notre-Dame went off with the precision of a military parade. The Bonaparte princesses raged at having to carry the train of the hated Josephine, but they created no scandal. Napoleon himself placed upon his head the crown, which was a replica of Charlemagne's; and it was he who crowned Josephine, as may be seen in David's admirable (and inaccurate) painting. The face of the Empress had been carefully made up by a noted painter, Isabey; and for her robes Chevalier, the court tailor, sent his bill amounting to 74,346 francs 74 centimes. The winter day was comparatively fair and mild. The procession, on its way back from Notre-Dame, took a wide swing by way of the Boulevards. The good people of Paris, who dearly love a pageant, had their fill.

The ceremony at Notre-Dame had a brilliant and fateful aftermath. So far Napoleon had not been fully committed to the extension of his rule beyond the "natural frontiers". The hold of France on the satellite republics —the Ligurian, Helvetic, Batavian—could have been gradually relaxed. But he had made himself President of the Italian (formerly Cisalpine) Republic; now he decided to be king of Italy (13 March, 1805), and, like his illustrious predecessor Charlemagne, to assume in Milan the Iron Crown of the Lombards (26 May). Piedmont had already been carved into French departments, and the Ligurian Republic craved the privilege of being absorbed. Thus Napoleon no longer was simply the sovereign of a vastly increased France: he was manifestly heading for the Empire of the West, of Europe, of the world.

Any permanent reconciliation with Austria was now out of the question. And every new annexation was another challenge to England; for although the Continental Blockade did not become a rigid system until the following year, already every port that passed under French control was closed to British commerce. Early in 1805 Russia, Austria, Great Britain, and Naples were preparing a new coalition. Even Spain, misruled by the Queen's favourite, Godoy, Prince of the Peace, was beginning to waver in her abject and ruinous subservience to France. Prussia was Yea-and-Nay: Queen Louise was ardently in favour of the Russian alliance; the weak-kneed King preferred to wait and rush to the aid of the victor, piously hoping it would not be Napoleon. The minor German states, technically Napoleon's allies, would gladly have followed Prussia's example.

The only open enemies, however, were England and her satellite Portugal. Against England, Napoleon made gigantic preparations for an invasion. He had immense forces gathered at and near Boulogne. It was there that they received the name of Grand Army; there also that the first decorations of the Legion of Honour were distributed. Thousands of flat landing boats were ready to transport the mighty host. All that Napoleon needed was control of the Channel for three days.

Napoleon had won victories against heavy odds: why should not his admiral, Latouche-Tréville or, after his death, Villeneuve, show the same daring and achieve the same success? What Napoleon refused to realize was that Carnot had handed him a magnificent instrument: there had been no Carnot for the navy. Armies can be improvised and prove effective, especially against cumbrous and tradition-ridden adversaries; but at sea there is no substitute for seamanship and gunnery. With all his unrivalled power of self-delusion, Napoleon must have known that his naval forces were no match, in sheer mass, equipment, command or training, for the fleets of Great Britain, unchallenged since the close of the American war. And Napoleon's ally, the Spanish fleet, was in even worse plight: a ruin barely kept afloat.

The plan evolved by Napoleon was so gigantic, so hazardous, so completely out of touch with reality, that historians have come to wonder whether it was not a titanic bluff. It was, more probably, a titanic gamble: there was a chance in a hundred that it might succeed. The French were to entice Nelson to the West Indies, as though their sole purpose was to reconquer Haiti and protect their other colonies. There they would elude him, and while he was playing blindman's buff in the Caribbean, they would sail full-speed for Europe, collect the various French and Spanish squadrons in Spanish ports, force the blockade of Brest, and sweep into the Channel, in full mastery for a fateful few days.

The whole fantastic scheme had collapsed even before Nelson destroyed the French and Spanish fleets at Trafalgar (21 October, 1805). The Grand Army had already left Boulogne. Napoleon received the news between two brilliant victories, Ulm and Austerlitz, and affected the most perfect equanimity. Trafalgar was not a decision, but a confirmation: the decision lay in the utter disparity of the two instruments. It deepened England's sense of her invincibility; yet William Pitt was soon to die in despair, and his successor Fox was a partisan of peace.

At Boulogne, Napoleon had been poised between two possibilities: a descent upon England, which was becoming more and more improbable, and a Continental war, which was growing into a very definite threat. In August the problem was decided for him: he received definite information that the Third Coalition was formed (it was signed on 9 August), and, on the 23rd, that Villeneuve was bottled up in Cádiz. On paper, the coalition was formidable; and it felt confident of success. But Naples was weak, Russia was far away, Austria was slow, Prussia was hesitating: a single swift blow could dislocate the loose and cumbrous alliance. One word of command: the Grand Army, two hundred thousand strong, turned away from the Channel, and in "seven torrents" rushed headlong towards Vienna.

This marks the beginning of the strictly Napoleonic wars, which were not to end until nine years later, in Paris, with a brief epilogue in 1815. It is a miracle that such an unequal conflict should have been protracted for a whole decade. The miracle was not altogether due to the genius of one man. Marshal Foch said: 'After commanding Allied armies, I am less impressed with Napoleon's victories.' Napoleon, sole ruler, sole commander, imposed upon his own forces, civil and military, an artificial but redoubtable unity. The Allies, richer in all resources, were divided, self-diffident, and mutually suspicious. After a decade of failure they were barely beginning to hope anew, when their smashing defeat at Austerlitz stunned them for years to come. It was the shadow of Austerlitz that weakened Napoleon's enemies at Jena, Friedland, and even Wagram.

Napoleon affected to believe that military prestige was indispensable to his rule. But if he thought that France *demanded* victories, he was only transferring his own inner flaw to the whole nation, and *at the time* he was wrong. In the resignation of the French to his rule there is no proof that the great pageant of martial glory played

an essential part. France, in 1805 as in 1799, was yearning
for peace. Most Frenchmen believed that the Allies
were the aggressors; but the renewal of the war
was received with dismay. Bonds fell again, though
Napoleon confidently promised a brief and victorious
campaign.

No doubt his contemporaries "cheered the team":
Paris hailed him on his return almost as deliriously as
New York greeted General Douglas MacArthur. But even
with the tumult and the shouting went shrugs of
increasing weariness: "Another victory: but where is
peace?" The *bourgeoisie*, most careful to preserve the *élite*
that formed the armature of France, bought themselves
off from military service. Among the common people,
the number of those who avoided conscription constantly
increased; the "grumbling" of the rank and file rose at
times to an ominous growl. It was only under Louis-
Philippe (1830-48), a régime dedicated to peace at any
price and to Business as the sole business of France,
that the French, in romantic reaction, went on a wild
spree of retrospective glory. At that time it was safe to
quaff the heavy wine—as of thirty years before. But when
Thiers, in 1840, engaged in a spirited and faintly
Napoleonic policy, he was rejected by King, Parliament,
bourgeoisie, and people. The proper place of an epic is
in the storied past.

The army that turned so smartly from Boulogne to
the upper Danube was indeed the Grand Army: not in
numbers merely, but in fighting quality. It was an army
led by young veterans: it had been fighting for ten years,
and most of its marshals were under forty. The spirit
varied with the ranks. The marshals themselves were
sated with glory and eager for enjoyment. They felt
themselves Napoleon's peers in age, origins, and ability;
and they hated the thought of risking for his sake all

their fabulous gains. Among those who served him best were many who were to betray him: Bernadotte, Ney, Marmont, Augereau. The common soldiers grumbled and were beginning to doubt. Pure Napoleonism was found, not among the marshals and not among the *grognards*, but among the officers. Some belonged to the aristocracy, the old fighting caste, for whom an army career was part of *noblesse oblige*. Others, on the contrary, loved the army because it was more democratic, truer to the spirit of the Revolution, than the stiff bureaucracy at home. For many, military life was the only way of escaping the infinite dullness, like a pall of lead, that the Empire was spreading over French society. To be an officer under Napoleon held the promise of gay adventure. It afforded full scope for the "triple talent" that the folk song ascribed to Henri IV: *"de boire et de se battre, et d'être un vert galant"* ("to drink, and to fight, and to be a very devil with the ladies").

We are told, and we easily believe, that Napoleon cherished his army: a craftsman loves his tools; and there is little doubt that he was a wonder of efficiency. Yet, to our surprise, even Napoleon-worshippers like Kircheisen and Madelin admit that the administrative departments of the army—the service of supplies, the paymaster, the sanitary formations—were woefully and even tragically inadequate.[1] The troops, and particularly the Guard, were given resplendent uniforms, which are still the delight of historical painters. But these were not renewed, and half-way through a campaign they were soiled and tattered. The pitiful pay was constantly in arrears. For food each unit had to prey on the local population; and when several corps in succession passed through the same countryside, the peasants were driven

[1] The authority on the subject, unchallenged, is J. Morvan: *Le Soldat Impérial* (2 vols., Paris, 1904-7).

to despair and the soldiers were starving. There were admirable surgeons like Larrey; but even in successful campaigns, the field hospitals were shambles. Posterity has chosen to ignore the seamy and nightmarish sides of Napoleonic warfare. So did the survivors: out of one million veterans, a few score wrote their memoirs, a whole generation after the events, at a time when the fashion was to revel in glory. Yet even in Coignet's artless *Notebooks*, the most engaging of all those documents, the grim reality appears under the grand parade.

Masséna, "the Darling of Victory", was holding Italy. The "seven torrents"—the corps of Bernadotte, Marmont, Davout, Soult, Lannes, Ney, and Augereau—were reaching the Danube; Murat's cavalry was dashing ahead; Napoleon himself was in reserve, with the Imperial Guard, "supreme hope and supreme thought".

In a few days the famed Austrian commander, Mack, was penned up in Ulm and compelled to surrender (17 October). On 14 November Napoleon was at Schönbrunn, the imperial palace near Vienna. The Austrian and Russian armies attempted to organize themselves for resistance in Moravia. There, on 2 December, the three Emperors joined in combat. The winter mists lifted at the right moment: it was "the sun of Austerlitz".

Austerlitz has been called "the most perfect battle in history": it certainly was Napoleon's masterpiece. He guessed every move of the enemies; he concealed every one of his own. When the seven-hour fighting was over, the Allies had lost 37,000 men, the French barely 8,000. In the snow that followed the brief outburst of sunshine, the Russian and Austrian Emperors were in headlong flight, their troops in abysmal confusion. No wonder the

conqueror was wildly acclaimed by his troops; no wonder
he addressed to them a ringing proclamation, a classic
of military eloquence. The anniversary of his coronation
could not have been celebrated with a more magnificent
festival of glory.

Napoleon granted the Russians a generous armistice—
too generous, in the opinion of some generals. Upon
helpless Austria he imposed a Draconian peace. Talleyrand had always advised moderation: he had long
believed that only with Austria as a contented
partner could a durable settlement in Europe be
attained. Napoleon swept the suggestion aside. No
concessions; a heavy war indemnity; territories for
his German allies, for Italy, for France. His Empire
now extended to the Illyrian Provinces, on the Adriatic,
stepping-stones towards that eternal mirage, Constantinople.

In 1805 Russia, still at war, had retired into her own
territory "to lick her wounds and weep for her dead".
England was incapable of effecting a landing: on the
Continent, Napoleon's fiat was law. Austerlitz intoxicated
him, as it crushed the spirit of his enemies. It focused
sharply in his mind the "Austerlitz complex", that one
good battle could solve every problem. It was an
Austerlitz that he kept seeking on his march to Moscow;
and as late as 1814, when he had won a partial success
in Champagne, he already imagined himself chasing the
enemies, helter-skelter, into the Siberian plains. Was he
not the victor of Austerlitz, "the god of Fortune and of
War"?

For a few months reality seemed to anticipate his
wildest dreams. As in an old-fashioned Christmas panto-
mime, wonders piled upon wonders. He could calmly
decree that the millennial Holy Roman Empire had
ceased to exist, and that the House of Bourbon no longer

reigned in Naples. He could distribute thrones to his clan: Murat, Grand Duke of Berg, Joseph, King of Naples, Louis, King of Holland, Jerome, King of Westphalia, Eliza, Princess of Piombino and Lucca, later Grand Duchess of Tuscany. He could create a Confederacy of the Rhine, with himself as Protector. He could confer royal titles upon the ancient dynasties of Germany, titles that they accepted with gratitude and preserved proudly until 1918. He could shift as he pleased the medieval shadows that had survived the Enlightenment; he gave no thought to the underlying reality, the interests and the will of the peoples.

The position of Prussia was still uncertain. Outwardly she had preserved neutrality, and the Prussian envoy went so far as to congratulate Napoleon on his victory. To bind Prussia to himself, Napoleon had promised her the Electorate of Hanover, but he felt under no obligation to such a shifty partner. It looked as though peace with Russia and England were within reach: in that case, Hanover would be restored to the King of England. Prussia, attempting to dupe everybody, felt duped in her turn, and bewildered. Fox, who wanted peace, died; the anti-Napoleonic coalition revived between England and Russia; Prussia, this time, was compelled to decide; and the torrents of the Grand Army swept over her.

In her own conceit, Prussia was still the finest military power in Europe. Her armies had withdrawn at Valmy (1792) for reasons of general policy: they had not considered themselves defeated. At every victory of the Revolutionary troops, the veterans of Old Fritz smiled: "Ah! But wait till we, the real soldiers, get into this fight!" The outcome was Jena and Auerstädt; the complete annihilation of the Prussian forces; fortresses surrendering to a squadron of hussars; the King and Queen of Prussia refugees under Russian protection. The French entered Berlin in triumph, Murat in the lead, with twenty thousand francs' worth of plumes; Napoleon, in dramatic contrast, with his riding coat of sober grey and with a penny cockade on his plain black hat.

Jena and Auerstädt offer a good illustration of Napoleon's skill as a self-advertiser. They were twin battles, fought on the same day, 14 October. At Auerstädt, Davout, with the smaller French force, defeated the main Prussian army. At Jena, Napoleon had the easier task. Auerstädt was unquestionably the more meritorious victory. Napoleon was not grudging in his praises of Davout: he made him later Duke of Auerstädt. Yet he contrived, for his contemporaries and for posterity, to create the impression that Jena was one of the decisive battles in world history, Auerstädt a minor engagement.

Russia was still unsubdued. The Battle of Eylau in East Prussia (7-8 February, 1807), in biting weather, was bloody and indecisive; the French held their ground, but they were too badly mauled to pursue the retreating enemy. Augereau, made the scapegoat, was sent back to Paris. Napoleon was held in check twelve hundred miles from his capital. The momentum of Austerlitz and Jena, however, kept up the spirit of the French and overawed the Germans: Napoleon could safely go into winter quarters in Warsaw and in the castles of Osterode and Finkenstein; and he managed gradually to replenish his army. Before Eylau, his supply system had broken down altogether, and the sufferings of the troops were indescribable.

Only on 14 June, 1807, at Friedland, was he able to inflict a severe defeat upon the Russians and the remnant of the Prussian forces. It was not an Austerlitz; still, it led the Russian generals to advise an armistice. Alexander, engaged in wars with Persia and with Turkey, was ready to come to terms. So, for once, was Napoleon: he had sent Duroc to offer peace. The two Emperors met at Tilsit on a raft moored in the Niemen. The Imperial Guards fraternized in Homeric banquets; the two autocrats embraced and swore eternal friendship. Alexander affirmed: 'I hate the British as bitterly as you do.' Russia was to join the Continental Blockade, which Napoleon had decreed in Berlin (21 November, 1806). So a personal meeting of the Big Two had settled the affairs of the world, with no regard for ideologies and sentimentalities. Napoleon could return to Paris in August, more than ever the conquering hero. He celebrated his victory in the most appropriate manner by suppressing the only institution where speech was still tolerated, the Tribunat.

It was during the winter lull before Friedland that Napoleon, in Warsaw, became acquainted with a Polish lady, Countess Marie Walewska. 'Talleyrand', he crudely said, 'got her for me.' The episode, however, was far more creditable than these brutal words would indicate. She was eighteen, her husband seventy; both ardent patriots, they hoped that the Man of Destiny would resurrect their country, obliterated twelve years before. Napoleon and Marie sincerely loved each other. But Napoleon was not the man to let his tender feelings interfere with political problems, and he continued to play fast and loose with Polish aspirations. The lovers met again in Vienna in 1809; their son, Alexander Colonna Walewski, was to have an honoured career under the Second Empire.

Meanwhile Napoleon was writing delightful letters to the Empress: "I love no woman except my little Josephine, good, sulky, and capricious." When she expressed the desire to join him, he put his imperial foot down: the place was cold, uncomfortable, barbarous, totally unfit for a delicate lady. Napoleon was by nature blunt; but even without Talleyrand's coaching he could also practise diplomacy.

CHAPTER SIX

DARK OMENS

1808—1809

AUSTERLITZ, Jena, Friedland: three decisive victories, three settlements imposed from a position of strength; and peace still a will-o'-the-wisp. A single voice heard; between outbursts of well-drilled applause, a vast silence, as if haunted by the ghosts of suppressed murmurings. The incredible adventure still incredible; yet the only actual, the only conceivable, reality.

England was now the sole enemy. Her Continental allies defeated, she remained impregnable. The Channel was a fact that Napoleon's imagination could not conjure away. So the Man of Arms, baffled, had to turn to an unfamiliar weapon, economics. It would be effective against "a nation of shopkeepers". On 16 May, 1806, Fox had declared a partial blockade of the northern European coast. On 21 November, 1806, in Berlin, Napoleon decreed that, in massive retaliation, all Europe be closed to British commerce. At Milan, on 17 December, 1807, the prohibition was made stricter, and neutrals were compelled to take sides.

If political and diplomatic issues are still cloudy after one hundred and fifty years, economic problems remain veiled in darkness absolute. Realities are confused, and only hypotheses can assume definiteness—in the realm of the might-have-been. The Berlin Decree possesses the

100

true Napoleonic style. It is still very impressive, but, like the elaborate constitution of the Empire, or the Imperial University, it was a façade, not "a mass of granite". Historians still affirm that through the blockade Napoleon *nearly* brought England to her knees: she suffered a severe economic crisis in 1811, with signs of mounting discontent. But the financial situation of France was even worse, and the discontent more profound.

Closing the Continent to British goods was bound to be a severe blow to a manufacturing and trading nation. Severe, but not fatal: Napoleon seems to have overlooked the fact that the rest of the world still existed. On the sea his fiat was not law. England maintained free intercourse with the Levant, India, the Far East. For a number of reasons her trade with America was hampered: Jefferson declared an embargo on 22 December, 1807. Canada as yet was of minor importance. But England had now access to the former colonies of Holland and of France, and to the vast Iberian world, ripe for expansion.

If the *mutual* blockade had been effective, it need not have strangled continental Europe either. At that time a European *autarky* or closed economy was not inconceivable. With proper communications and no artificial barriers, Europe could have fed herself. She had all the mineral resources for her immediate needs. Only two vital articles came from beyond the sea: cotton and sugar. But wool, hemp, flax and silk were available, and the beet-sugar industry was created, which survived the emergency. No satisfactory substitute for coffee was discovered: the use of chicory is a lamentable legacy of those far-off unhappy days. But coffee-drinking in Europe was less than two hundred years old: Mme de Sévigné had pronounced it a fad. No proud nation will ever surrender for lack of coffee.

The economic cold war could therefore have been

prolonged for decades without bringing disaster to either side. It represented simply the protectionist ideal carried to an extreme. Now protection makes the weak more anaemic, but does not kill them outright; and it seems to strengthen the strong. England's maritime predominance was built up, for two centuries, through the Navigation Act. One thing is certain: economic warfare *per se* could not have secured a clear-cut political decision. England and the Continent might have snarled at each other over the fence for ages and been only a little the worse for it. If Napoleon did fail, it was because he mismanaged Continental affairs.

But the fact we are liable to forget is that the blockade, while by no means a farce or a mirage, was very far from being a solid reality. The Master of Europe issued commands with the majesty of omnipotence, and his imperial gesture was duly recorded. But he did not continuously hold that fatiguing Jove-like pose. Smuggling assumed grandiose proportions, and Napoleon winked at it. Furthermore, both he and the British granted a fantastic number of licences to trade with the enemy. The conditions of that authorized illegal trade were debated in "open secret" negotiations. While the licences alleviated the hardships of industrialists and consumers, they brought profits to the hungry imperial treasury and to a long series of officials and financiers. For a licence to trade was an asset that itself became an object of trade. It was because of his well-known connections with England that the speculator Ouvrard could be Fouché's agent in surreptitious peace feelers. There was an International of Finance, in Amsterdam, Hamburg, Frankfurt, in close contact with London and Paris. Hope, Labouchère, Parish, Baring, were among its leaders. And especially the Rothschilds, whose empire came into being in those days: an empire *ære perennius,* more durable than

Napoleon's bronze. *Homo economicus* is wiser than *Homo politicus,* and especially than *Homo pugnax.*

The Continental Blockade involved Napoleon in a series of high-handed acts. We should not believe, however, that he had a monopoly of brutality: England's treatment of Copenhagen, for instance, in 1801 and in 1807, was also an unscrupulous abuse of force. Both the British lion and the French eagle were beasts of prey. The blockade served as a last-minute pretext for intervention in the Papal States. It was to spell the doom of the short-lived Kingdom of Holland under Napoleon's own brother Louis. Ultimately, it led the Empire to stretch out absurd tentacles: the Hansa Towns, Bremen, Hamburg, Lübeck, became French cities. Yet these moves, at the same time irresponsible and logical, were of secondary importance compared with the repeated redrawing of the European map to suit the Master's interests, his fancies, or his whims. Although they caused severe hardships to certain commercial interests, they were not so keenly felt as the constant ubiquitous drain of gold and men which was the essence of the Napoleonic system. We may go farther: blockade, tribute, and conscription, heavy as they were, were secondary grievances compared with the humiliation imposed by the Master upon his allies, even upon his own brothers, as well as upon his enemies. Every word of adulation from reluctant lips, every benefit contemptuously tossed by him, would swell the treasure of hate in the secret of the hearts. Realists knew long before Sir Norman Angell that war never pays: the sole cause of war is wounded pride. And it was Napoleon's fate to wound the pride of all in order to prove to himself that he was the Great Ruler of the Great Nation. It was his mad wager with Destiny.

.   .   .   .   .

The conflict with the Pope became acute in 1808. It was the first, perhaps the decisive sign that the imperial system was unsound. The quarrel was caused only in a small degree by the Continental Blockade: Civitavecchia was but a minor port. It had started earlier, at the very moment when the Concordat was promulgated. In fact, as we have seen, it started with Constantine.

This age-long conflict was complicated by an absurdity of long standing: the Holy Father was also an Italian princeling. As such, he had to play Peninsular and European politics on the most cynical Machiavelian plane. A Pope advised His Most Christian Majesty the King of France to seek the support of the Grand Turk against His Most Catholic and Apostolic Majesty the Holy Roman Emperor. This was in early Renaissance days: three centuries later the confusion still prevailed. So there arose from Rome four voices, seldom in full accord: that of the Holy Father in his spiritual character; that of the bewildered sovereign of the puny Papal States; that of Pius VII the man, meek, long-suffering, with a lingering affection for Napoleon; and that of the Curia, hating the usurper and all his works. And Napoleon was not a single entity either. There were in him the "Man of God" who had restored religion; but also the heir of the Gallican kings, the disciple of the Enlightenment, the soldier of the Revolution, and most of all the insatiable egotist who considered dissent a personal affront.

Thus, as Napoleon entered Schönbrunn in November 1805, he received from the Pope an ultimatum demanding the evacuation of Ancona. Napoleon shrugged the request away: Austerlitz was a sufficient answer. Then, in 1806, Pius VII refused to recognize Joseph as King of Naples: according to tradition, only the Holy See could bestow that crown. 'But I am the Emperor of Rome!' Napoleon asserted. 'There is no Emperor of Rome,' the

Pope replied. 'The Pontiff wields full sovereign power in the City.' Napoleon was already thinking of "withdrawing from the Papacy the donation made by his illustrious predecessor Charlemagne".

On 12 November, 1806, Napoleon, from Berlin, ordered the Pope to join his Italian Confederacy: thus his Kingdom of Italy would be linked with his brother's Kingdom of Naples. The Pope demurred. In the summer of 1807 he was intimidated into joining the Continental Blockade. But Napoleon wanted more: a full promise that the Pope would in all cases make common cause with the Emperor. This meant undisguised vassalage; nerved to resistance by the Curia, Pius VII refused (12 December, 1807). Thereupon, on 12 January, 1808, Napoleon ordered General Miollis to march on Rome. Every protest was met by another turn of the screw. A first excommunication (27 May, 1808) was not made public. On 12 May, 1809, came the outright annexation of the Papal States; on 10 June, a formal excommunication; on 6 July, the Pontiff was wrenched from the Holy City and imprisoned, at Grenoble, Savona, Fontainebleau. Even though the climax was deferred, the essential facts were known throughout Europe; and they were to have a decisive influence on the turn of affairs in Spain.

The Spanish entanglement was to prove an incurable wound: while the Emperor was still winning victories and annexing far-off lands, his strength and prestige were slowly bleeding in the Peninsula. This tragic adventure, into which Napoleon seemed urged by the demon of self-destruction, was preceded by a sort of rehearsal, the conquest of Portugal. That expedition appeared logical enough, as logic goes in such affairs. England was inexpugnable; but she had two dependencies on the

mainland which an enemy could seize as hostages. One
was the Electorate of Hanover, the personal possession of
the English King. The second was Portugal. Ever since
the Methuen Treaty (1703)—in form a mere commercial
arrangement for preferential tariffs on wines and woollens
—Portugal had been in fact a most docile satellite of
England.

Before the expedition could start, complicated negotiations were necessary with Spain, whose territory had to
be traversed. Portugal was neatly partitioned on paper.
There would be, as a commission, a principality for
Godoy, the Spanish minister. Another slice would go to
the Infanta Maria Luisa in exchange for the Kingdom
of Etruria, which Napoleon had seized. The rest might
be the booty of the French commander, Junot. Junot was
a harum-scarum swashbuckler with a spotted record; but,
a devouted retainer ever since the siege of Toulon, he
was one of Napoleon's personal favourites. He had
courted two of the Bonaparte princesses—perhaps a
doubtful claim to a crown; and he had married into a
family, the Permons, whom Napoleon knew and
respected.

Junot's advance was a victory of luck over inefficiency.
The Grand Army, in central Europe, was claiming the
best in troops, officers, equipment: Junot was given only
untrained recruits. The winter march through the mountains broke their fragile morale; soon there were more
stragglers than combatants. Barely five thousand soldiers,
starving and in rags, reached Abrantes, the fortified town
that guarded the Tagus valley and the road to Lisbon. A
show of resistance could have swept back that tatter-
demalion host. But the royal House of Braganza had
already taken flight to Brazil; Junot entered the capital
a few hours after they had left. He was made Duke of
Abrantes; but he never became King Andoche I; he never

won even his marshal's baton. But for a while he strutted
right royally in his good city, a duodecimo Napoleon.
Six years later Junot, demented, jumped out of a window.

Napoleon accused Talleyrand of having trapped him
into the Spanish embroilment: as in the case of the Duke
of Enghien, no conclusive evidence remains. Melodramatic history would like to imagine Napoleon, whose
thought was lightning and whose deeds were thunder-
bolts, suddenly deciding to establish his rule in Spain;
and the Spanish people, with the same instant determination, rising at once in desperate resistance. Once again,
plain history offers a more complex and blurred
picture. The Spanish affair had been under way ever
since 1795.

The Spanish Bourbons had been among the most
ardent crusaders again regicide France. But the young
Republic, after early reverses, had rallied on all fronts;
beyond the Pyrenees, the French invaded Catalonia and
the Basque Provinces. By the Treaty of Basel (1795),
Spain had to pay ransom for her losses with her half of
Santo Domingo. The royal house affected to be well
satisfied with the outcome, and the all-powerful minister
Godoy was created "Prince of the Peace".

In 1796 Spain joined France in the fight against
England: as in the War of the Spanish Succession, as in
the War of American Independence, a familiar pattern,
almost a tradition. But in this ill-fated alliance, Spain was
constantly the loser. Napoleon demanded Louisiana back
—and sold it to Jefferson for a song. The miserable
squadrons of Spain were buffeted in every encounter,
badly mauled at Cape St. Vincent in 1797, destroyed
at Trafalgar in 1805. Napoleon had a short way with
satellites: they were taught to pay, and serve, and
claim no rewards. How the Spanish people, famed for

punctilious pride, could endure the French yoke for
twelve aching years truly passeth all understanding.
Evidently there were treasures of fatalistic apathy in
that country capable of the fiercest reactions. And,
although this very important element is hard to gauge,
there were liberal tendencies in Spain willing to link
their fate with the principles of 1789. Charles III had been
an enlightened despot. He had expelled the Jesuits. This
afrancesado or Frenchified element was not large, but it
had vigour and intelligence. These advocates of renova-
tion might sincerely have collaborated with a liberal
France; but they had almost lost heart by the time
Napoleon directly intervened.

The key of the situation was the royal family, Charles
IV and Maria Luisa of Parma, his Queen. A caricatural
pair; the King weak of mind and will, his consort a
harridan. Goya seems to have caught their spirit in court
portraits which might almost figure among his nightmarish *Caprichos*. The Queen imposed upon the realm
her paramour, Godoy, a handsome guardsman, univer-
sally hated and despised. Godoy was no convinced Franco-
phile: in 1805 he was ready to throw in his lot with the
Third Coalition. But threats and bribes kept him in line.
The horrible *ménage à trois* was a secret to no one except
perhaps Charles IV. Ferdinand, the heir apparent, was
aware of it. He became the centre of a diffused opposition
against Godoy, against his own parents, and against
France, whose puppets they were.

This spirit of discontent was manifested in an uprising
at Aranjuez (17 March, 1808) directed against Godoy.
Finally the crisis broke out in the royal family itself.
Mother and son hurled violent accusations at each other,
and Charles IV, in bewilderment and despair, signed his
abdication. Godoy could have been made the only scapegoat: the new King, Ferdinand VII, confiscated his property

amid universal rejoicing. Ferdinand himself was no pattern
of patriotism and dignity. In his rage against Godoy, he
was eager to enlist the favour of the French Protector.
He humbly begged for the hand of any Napoleonic
princess. A daughter of Lucien was brought to Paris
with that end in view; but as she was found tainted
with her father's "Jacobinism", she was sent back to
Rome.

The French were already in Spain, on their way to
Portugal. Murat, with "an army of observation", was
advancing into the distracted country, and reached
Madrid on 23 March, 1808. He had no authority to
recognize the new King. He advised the royal family to
seek Napoleon's arbitration; and the trio proceeded
to Bayonne. The irrepressible Godoy was there ahead of
them : he was to remain "attached" to his master and to
his mistress until their deaths.

Napoleon welcomed father, mother, and son with
gently smiling jaws. They were moved to tears by the
kindness and courtesy of their glorious and omnipotent
ally. After a family dinner on 1 May, a reconciliation
seemed to be effected. Charles IV would resume the
crown, and Napoleon, the family arbiter, would more
than ever be the actual ruler of Spain.

But on 2 May, in Madrid, as two more members
of the royal family were preparing to leave for
Bayonne, the mob rose in protest, with a rage that was a
portent. On the Spanish side, there had been no preparations; Murat, sensing trouble, was ready. Indeed, he
would have welcomed this occasion to impose his will.
Had not Napoleon written to Joseph, King of Naples,
two years before : "Shoot down those *lazzaroni* without
pity. You can keep an Italian population in its place only
through holy fear"? For "Italian", "Spanish" would read
just as well. A few whiffs of grapeshot, and order reigned

in Madrid. Only this chaotic, this abortive *Dos de Mayo* had long and tragic repercussions. It revealed to the Spanish people the fierceness of its own temper. On that day, war in the spirit was declared; and it was to be implacable.

The news infuriated Napoleon: somehow he made the Bourbons responsible for the (misguided) loyalty of their people. The epilogue of the tragi-comedy was hurried through. Ferdinand returned the crown to his father, who abdicated in favour of Napoleon. The princes were sent to France as guests of honour, not as prisoners. Their host, at the Château of Valençay, was no less a personage than Maurice de Talleyrand-Périgord, Prince of Benevento, recently promoted to Vice Grand Elector. ('The only vice,' Fouché remarked, 'that he was still lacking.') The Princess of Benevento was expected to entertain her guests to the best of her well-known abilities. Napoleon was a most considerate jailer.

Murat, Grand Duke of Berg, expected to become king: he was on the spot, and a vigorous soldier. Napoleon hesitated. He offered the heavy crown to Louis, who wisely declined; then to Joseph, who accepted with reluctance. In a peaceful country, Joseph might have been an excellent constitutional sovereign: in the inferno of Spain his moderation was interpreted as weakness, and his lack of military talent made him the merest lay figure. Out of 120 Spanish notables summoned to Bayonne, only 40 appeared. They enthusiastically endorsed Napoleon's choice; and, for good measure, they ratified a constitution which was to remain stillborn. This was on 6 June: the spirit of the *Dos de Mayo* had spread throughout the land. When he reached his capital, King Joseph was supported by a handful of *afrancesados* and at war with the rest of his people.

There were two main causes for this nation-wide, spontaneous insurrection. The first is best expressed in the homely phrase: "the last straw". For ten years at least, Spain had suffered from France's high-handedness; the farce at Bayonne brought the final revulsion. The second was the hold the clergy had on a fanatically Catholic population; even Belgium, Bavaria, and Rome were tepid in comparison. Had Napoleon presented himself with the nimbus the Concordat had given him, his chances would have been great: on 2 December, 1804, he had become the Lord's Anointed. But in 1808, although the full details were not divulged, the masses felt, and the priests knew, that the Emperor was irremediably at odds with the Pope. So far Napoleon had fought dynasts: now he had to face both a faith and a people. The Spanish conflict assumed at once that character of sombre ferocity which is inseparable from religious wars.

The French were not yet taking seriously that loose uprising of priests and peasants. Dupont, a commander with an excellent reputation, was sent to subdue Andalusia, in the far south. He reported at first that the operation was a mere military march. He must have proceeded with incredible carelessness; and it was said that he was hampered by wagon-loads of booty. On 19 June, at Baylen, he was attacked on two sides by insurgent forces. He thought himself surrounded, and capitulated at once. Furthermore, he included in the surrender his detached subordinates, who were in no danger. The French were to have been allowed to retire with arms and baggage. But the insurgents were not conventional fighters: they treated Dupont's troops as prisoners and huddled them into an island camp, where most of them perished of callous neglect.

The effect of Baylen was enormous throughout Spain

and throughout Europe. Indeed, the disgraceful episode might be called one of the decisive battles in history. It was an Austerlitz in reverse: it pricked the bubble of French invincibility. The *Dos de Mayo* spirit received its confirmation on the battlefield. Portugal and England struck an alliance with Spain, represented by a junta operating from Cádiz. Sir Arthur Wellesley, the future Duke of Wellington, landed in the Peninsula. Joseph fled from Madrid in a panic. Junot, with his scarecrow army, found himself isolated in Portugal, and lost heart. He capitulated at Cintra (30 August). The British honourably carried out the terms of the convention; they shipped Junot and his men back to France.

Napoleon's rage may well be imagined. Baylen was not a mere defeat: he called it "a stain". Before he could proceed to Spain, he found it more essential than ever to strengthen his bond with Alexander of Russia. A meeting had been arranged at Erfurt. For nearly three weeks (27 September to 14 October) Napoleon displayed his power with deliberate ostentation. He appeared as the suzerain of the West, with kings and grand dukes in his train. Diplomatic conferences alternated with magnificent parties. The Comédie Française played before an audience of crowned heads. When the line was uttered:

"A great man's friendship is a boon from the gods",

Alexander effusively pressed Napoleon's hand. There was hunting on the battlefield of Jena; and, in better taste, a visit to Weimar, the capital of the German spirit. Goethe and Wieland were treated with greater honours than if they had been victorious commanders. The Treaty of Tilsit was formally confirmed. Yet Napoleon could feel a reticence that might easily turn into resistance and even enmity. Both autocrats were aware that Baylen had blotted out Friedland.

What Napoleon did not know was that Talleyrand was deliberately working against him. The great diplomat was no longer Minister of Foreign Affairs. This, however, implied no disgrace. Talleyrand himself had coveted one of the Grand Dignities of the Empire; and Napoleon had made it a rule that such exalted titles were incompatible with a cabinet position. But while the colourless Champagny was holding the portfolio, Talleyrand was still a trusted adviser, and he was brought to Erfurt in that confidential capacity. He told Alexander in plain terms: 'France is not interested in any conquest beyond the Rhine, the Alps, and the Pyrenees. The nation is civilized: her ruler is not.' And he adjured the Czar to save Europe and France by not committing himself irrevocably to Napoleon. It was the truth, and it took courage to utter it. It would have taken heroism to speak with the same definiteness to Napoleon. Talleyrand was no hero.

Napoleon rushed back from Erfurt to Paris, and from Paris to Spain. He had now a large army in the Peninsula, and some of his ablest lieutenants. A charge of the Polish light horse in the Somosierra Pass opened the way to Madrid. On 4 December, 1808, the Emperor entered the sullen city, and subjected it to a most rigorous state of siege. As a gesture of liberation, he abolished the Inquisition, the very name of which filled the French with horror. Fifty years before, Spain might have accepted such a reform from her own Charles III; in 1808 it seemed as though the persecutor of the Pope, the Antichrist, were of malice prepense destroying the very bulwark of Spanish faith.

Never was Napoleon swifter, and never more ruthless.

H

On 22 December he left Madrid to chase the British under
Sir John Moore. He crossed the Sierra de Guadarrama
in a terrific snowstorm; it was there that he heard curses
from his hard-driven soldiers. Relentlessly he pursued
the enemies towards Galicia; he was hoping to destroy
them altogether. Abruptly, at Astorga, he turned the
command over to Soult; and after a brief pause at
Valladolid, sped to Paris.

Soult did not have Napoleon's daimonic drive; he
gave the British time to embark at Coruña, where Sir
John Moore fell. In the meantime Palafox was holding
Saragossa against the French in one of the most heroic
and most atrocious sieges in history. Priests and women
were active in the defence and were mowed down in the
house-to-house fighting. Lannes, a hard-bitten soldier,
retched at the necessity of killing so many brave combatants. Finally, on 21 February, 1809, the garrison gave
up and was allowed to march out of the devastated city
with the honours of war. Large-scale resistance was
broken; King Joseph reigned in Madrid; but the *Dos de
Mayo* spirit was not quenched, and the stain of Baylen
was not effaced.

The news that caused Napoleon to leave his army
at Astorga was ominous indeed. He was informed that
in Paris a conspiracy was afoot, involving the most
powerful personages in the Empire; and that, three years
after the crushing blow of Austerlitz, Austria was again
preparing for war.

Parisian society had been amazed when, on 20
December, 1808, Fouché and Talleyrand appeared arm-
in-arm at a reception. Both knew the inner weaknesses of
the Empire as Napoleon never did. Neither wanted—as
yet—to destroy the régime; both had become convinced
that the Emperor was rushing into self-destruction. They

were "alerted". Their conjunction was rightly considered as a portent.

Their "conspiracy", however, was so far innocent enough. The same situation existed as at the time of Marengo. The whole state apparently depended upon one life, and that life precarious, at the mercy of dagger or bomb, stray bullet or germ. It was the duty of true statesmen to prepare for such an emergency. Joseph, who might have been a decent fair-weather head of the state, would never do in a desperate crisis. France was geared to military rule: Fouché and Talleyrand were in quest of a soldier whose stature would not seem comical by the side of Napoleon's. They thought of Moreau and of Bernadotte; at this time their choice fell on Murat. To what extent the *beau sabreur* King of Naples was aware of their preparations remains clouded. Certain it is that the ambition of his wife, Caroline, was as devouring as Napoleon's own.

All this was not openly disloyal: still, the fate of the Empire had been discussed behind Napoleon's back, and his disappearance coolly envisaged. Napoleon was angered by what he surmised even more than by what he knew. He chose to overlook Fouché's part in the plot: his threats to the Minister of Police were indirect, allusive. His wrath fell on Talleyrand alone, though he was still ignorant of the Erfurt betrayal. Cursing himself for his Spanish blunder, he made Talleyrand the scapegoat. The storm broke on 28 January, 1809, when Napoleon, a master of vigorous language, called his Vice Grand Elector and Grand Chamberlain 'S—t in a silk stocking'. He attempted to cap this unforgettable phrase with a more unforgivable insult: 'You did not tell me that the Duke of San Carlos was your wife's lover.' With Old World courtliness, Talleyrand replied: 'Sire, I did not think that this bit of information had anything to do with

Your Majesty's glory, or with mine.' He had stood his ground very well; still, he was sick with a fever all the next day. Even then Napoleon was of two minds about Talleyrand. He deprived him of his court functions and of the handsome income they carried; but he did not destroy him, or even discard him. Talleyrand remained Prince of Benevento, Vice Grand Elector, an ornament to the Empire.

History is at times repetitious to the verge of the ludicrous: Austria was arming again. She would not have dared to do so if, as Napoleon had a right to expect, Alexander had exerted a restraining influence: Napoleon was forced to realize that Tilsit and Erfurt had lost their virtue. So, with quiet intensity, he made his own preparations. No easy task: for now some of his best troops were in Spain. On 12 April, 1809, he was informed that Austria had declared war: within two hours he was leaving for Vienna. Within a month, after a short bombardment, he was entering the Austrian capital again.

But the Austrian army was intact in the field; and this time he had to face the best of the Austrian generals, Archduke Charles. Attempting to cross the Danube, Napoleon's troops were sharply defeated at Aspern and Essling and compelled to retire to the Lobau Island (21 May). The collapse of a bridge had caused a fatal shortage of ammunition.

For seven weeks Napoleon was held in check and practically hemmed in, a thousand miles from his capital; with the Pope's curse on his head, England unsubdued, Spain smouldering, Russia enigmatic, his German allies wavering. The news of Aspern-Essling, greatly amplified, spread a wild surmise throughout Europe: could the end be near at hand? Both the spirit of the Revolution and the national sentiment, a form of romanticism, had wakened the politically slumbrous mid-Continent. In

that welter of ideals Napoleon's reckless despotism acted
as a catalyst: *he* was the arch enemy of freedom in
every form. The whole of central Europe was in a
ferment. Andreas Hofer was rousing the Tyrol against
Franco-Bavarian rule. Colonel Dörnberg attempted to
overthrow Jerome in Westphalia. Major von Schill, a
Prussian, led an attack on Magdeburg and, after wild
forays, was finally captured at Stralsund. The dispossessed
Duke of Brunswick formed a volunteer corps and, in
connection with Austria, played havoc with Napoleon's
German allies. He managed to extricate himself and to
embark for England.

Napoleon was a gambler, but a cool-headed one. He
knew that delay was hurting his prestige; but he also
knew that a major defeat, so eagerly expected by all his
enemies, would be final. So he perfected his preparations with masterly patience. By 4 July he had one
hundred thousand men ready on Lobau, with over five
hundred guns and, this time, ample ammunition. Five
bridges had been built over the Danube. He had with
him his stars, Masséna and Davout; and by their side
Macdonald, Marmont, Oudinot, Bernadotte. On 6 July
the Battle of Wagram was won. It had been as bitterly
contested as Eylau: the French suffered greater losses
than the Austrians. A notable victory no doubt, a
masterpiece of tactics: still it was not an Austerlitz.
On the 15th, Napoleon was again in *his* palace of
Schönbrunn.

Napoleon was in no position to dictate. He was only
too ready to listen to the propositions of Metternich, the
Austrian Chancellor, just entering upon his forty years
of rule. Considering the military situation after Wagram,
the treaty signed at Schönbrunn on 14 October seems
extraordinarily harsh: Austria lost more territory—she
was completely cut off from the Adriatic—had to reduce

her army, was made to pay a heavy indemnity. Metternich
accepted those terms because he considered this merely
as a move in a long game. Austria had already signed
three treaties with France, at Campoformio in 1797, at
Lunéville in 1801, at Pressburg in 1805; she was ready to
sign a fourth "just as good". For the time being, at any
rate, Austria chose to side with the conqueror. Wagram
was a Friedland : the defeated had lost a battle, not the
war. Why not a Tilsit, a reconciliation, an alliance? It is
not certain that Metternich's game was then quite clear
in his own mind. With inflexible tendencies—the dynastic
state, a balanced cosmopolitan Europe, no democratic or
nationalistic nonsense—he was in the conduct of affairs a
thorough opportunist. He would play the French card,
in tolerably good faith, or the Russian card, or the
British card, provided that Austria would ultimately
be the gainer. He preserved that poker face until
1813.

An epilogue to the great crisis was almost an anti-
climax. Three weeks after Wagram—at least six weeks
too late—the British effected a landing on Walcheren
Island, at the mouth of the Scheldt. It was a most
ambitious enterprise : forty-two men-of-war escorted four
hundred transports carrying over forty thousand men.
The aim was to capture Antwerp. The danger was very
real: the strongly Catholic Belgian departments had
become dissatisfied as a result of the conflict between the
Pope and the Emperor. They would offer little resistance
to invasion; indeed, an uprising was not out of
the question. The regular French armies were either
fighting in Spain or watching an uneasy truce near
Vienna.

The great personages of the Empire, the stately Arch
Chancellor Cambacérès first among them, did not lose
their heads, but declined to use them. Trained to passive

obedience, they supinely waited for orders. Fouché alone
proved capable of action. At the time, he was acting
Minister of the Interior as well as Minister of Police. He
took hold of the situation with something of his old
Jacobin vigour. He issued proclamations in which
patriotism had almost a republican ring. He mobilized
the National Guard, officered by men who were not blind
devotees of Napoleon. He reassured the country; but he
demonstrated thereby that France was more than the
Emperor and could save herself in his absence. This
was *lèse-majesté*, and a crime that Napoleon could not
forgive.

Fouché went farther. After some misunderstanding at
Wagram, Bernadotte had left in a huff. He had never
been manageable, and in politics he was an uncertain
factor. But Marshall Bernadotte, Prince of Pontecorvo,
closely connected with the Bonaparte family, had at
least an impressive name. Fouché placed him at the
head of the military preparations. The two formed an
able team. Nothing could be more displeasing to the
Master.

By the time the Emperor returned, the danger had
vanished. The Earl of Chatham and Marshal Bernadotte
were not to cross swords. As Leclerc in Haiti was defeated
by fever, so Chatham on Walcheren was checked by a
milder form of the disease. He had hoped at least to
maintain a "pocket" at Flushing; but even this toe-hold
had to be abandoned. By 21 September the last British
troops had been evacuated. The fiasco was monumental
and complete.

Napoleon was of two minds. He upbraided the
dignitaries and ministers for their spinelessness. He duly
commended Fouché's energy. At the same time he made
light of the peril and hinted that the heroics of the
National Guard had a touch of the ridiculous. He fully

realized, however, how dangerous Fouché and Bernadotte could be. They might work with him, and work well; but not for him. They were not his men. In 1810 both of them were removed from the centre of French affairs. But they had not surrendered, and both of them still had the power to thwart Napoleon.

CHAPTER SEVEN

SPLENDOURS AND MISERIES

1810—1811

1810: never had the young Empire looked more impressive. What if it had received a severe wound at Trafalgar in 1805, a worse one at Baylen in 1808? It still seemed to be marching from strength to strength, from glory to glory.

A faith or a nation can stand crushing blows, for they live in the spirit. All régimes, however, are frail because they are machines; and a personal régime is frailest of all. Had Napoleon's miraculous luck held for a few more years, he might have found his Moscow in Samarkand, his Waterloo in Trebizond: by whatever name, the appointment could not be eluded. The Empire could not endure, because the Empire was Napoleon's dream, a dream that spurned every curb. At St. Helena, evoking the magic days of his early Italian victories, he said—magnificently, for his genius flashed in words of flame as well as in commands on the battlefield: 'I foresaw what I might become: I could see the world moving under me, as though I were borne aloft in the air.' A glorious vision: and lo, it was a vision. Napoleon constantly attempted to translate it into reality, to arrest its flight, to pin it down to earth. His institutions were meant to be anchors; he whose destiny was the insatiable quest yearned for stability.

So the great solipsist ("I, myself, alone, and that suffices!") was craving to perpetuate his name, his rule, his seed, for a thousand years. He refused to accept physical death: he wanted desperately to survive in the flesh. His own kin had disappointed him: the crowned Bonapartes, Joseph, Louis, Jerome, Caroline, could cease to be puppets only by opposing him; and when they did so, they became odious. He wanted a son of his own loins, the son Josephine had not been able to give him. He knew that the responsibility was not his. He had deliberately made the experiment; the chosen instrument was a reader in Caroline's household, Mlle Denuelle de la Plaigne. On 13 December, 1807, a man child was born to him, that pathetic Count Leon who, after a raffish career, was to die obscure and a pauper in 1881.

The problem of his succession had haunted him ever since the creation of the Empire. Josephine was aware of it, but she could not avert the blow. It is in his relations with her that Napoleon appears at his most natural and best. If it had not been for dynastic reasons, he would have been content to keep her by his side. For years he resisted the thought of a divorce, urged not by the Bonapartes only, but by Fouché. When he told her of his decision, she fainted. Bausset, the secretary who carried her away in his arms, testifies that the swooning was a bit of play-acting: historical characters are constantly on the stage. But even though her grief was slightly touched up for effect, it was none the less sincere. So was Napoleon's. He behaved with the utmost consideration and generosity: he was no Henry VIII. She retained the title of Empress, and was granted a dazzling allowance, which, of course, proved inadequate. The Senate was officially consulted. Eugene, unswerving in his devotion to his stepfather, gave the only speech in favour of the Emperor's resolve. The august assembly, not quite unanimously, ratified it (16 December, 1809), and Josephine left for La Malmaison.

To persuade the Senate was easy enough. But there had been a religious ceremony on the eve of the coronation. Rome alone could pronounce an annulment; and the Pope was at war with the Emperor. Napoleon's power over the French episcopate was still so great, however, that a solution was devised: even canon law may yield a painful inch to the successor of Constantine and Charlemagne. On 12 January, 1810, the *Officialité*, or Metropolitan's Court of Paris, declared itself competent. Cardinal Fesch and the witnesses, Berthier, Duroc, and Talleyrand, testified that the ceremony on 1 December, 1804, had not been a proper marriage; and so the religious bond was declared non-existent. Confident of the outcome, Napoleon had already gone a-wooing.

His choice was limited to the highest ruling families. He was not moved by the parvenu's desire to marry above his origins: he had reached the summit. Daughters of minor German royalties were considered and rejected: they were good enough only for the lesser members of the imperial connection—Jerome, Eugene, Berthier. One faction—Fouché and Caulaincourt among them—were advising a Russian marriage. Another favoured Austria. Napoleon was won over to the Russian side. There was a formal alliance between the two states, and a personal friendship between the two rulers. No ideological gulf separated them. If Alexander was an autocrat, so was Napoleon; and the Czar was rather more open to liberal ideas than the French Emperor. Napoleon was ready to make heavy sacrifices in order to retain Alexander's friendship. He formally repudiated any intention of reviving Poland: Marie Walewska's immolation had been of no avail. Caulaincourt, the French Ambassador, was instructed to sue for the hand of the

Czar's sister. At the news, which was not unexpected, the whole Russian imperial family was horror-stricken. In their eyes, the Great Friend and Ally was Antichrist. Moreover, Alexander had heeded Talleyrand's words at Erfurt. So he gave an evasive answer, which to Napoleon's ears sounded plain enough. A few days later Russia was courteously informed that the Emperor of the French had chosen an Austrian princess. The Romanovs, after all, were upstarts by the side of the Habsburgs.

To the Habsburgs, Napoleon's figure was even more horrific than to the Romanovs. They had suffered more at his hands; and he was at the head of the nation that had martyred one of their own, Marie-Antoinette, never professing repentance. Young Archduchess Marie-Louise, in particular, had been brought up in the detestation of the monster. But the destinies of Austria were in the hands of Metternich. In the masterly game he was playing, he would sacrifice a princess as if she were a pawn. Using Hymen as an instrument of national policy was deep in the Austrian tradition. There was an oft-quoted Latin distich with the key words: *Tu, felix Austria, nube:* "Let others do the fighting: thou, lucky Austria, wed." On 11 March, 1810, the marriage by proxy was celebrated in Vienna. Marie-Louise had been carefully brought up: she accepted her fate with quiet dignity. The classical-minded alluded to Iphigenia, to Jephthah's daughter; some spoke of "a beautiful heifer led to the sacrificial altar".

Beautiful she was not. As haughtily indifferent to all ideas as her great-aunt Marie-Antoinette, she possessed neither her spirit nor her charm. Yet this outrageous marriage of convenience was to take an unexpected turn. The Imperator, the incarnation of the state, the demigod, feeling the approach of middle age, desired passionately to be human at last, merely human. He was as impatient to be with his young wife as if he had been a second lieutenant. Throwing protocol to the winds, he rushed out to meet her ahead of the appointed place. He jumped into her carriage, kissed her ardently, and that same night, at Compiègne, claimed his marital rights. The strangely assorted pair were surprised and delighted with each other. Marie-Louise found that the Minotaur was a very affectionate monster. And Napoleon would gleefully tell his courtiers: 'Marry German girls! Nothing like them: healthy, honest, wholesome, and fresh as roses!'

The wedding ceremonies were of unparalleled splendour. The civil one took place at Saint-Cloud on 1 April, the religious one the next day in the Louvre; it was again performed by Uncle Fesch. There was one shadow in the rejoicings: out of thirty-nine stalls reserved for cardinals, twenty-one were left empty. The absentees were severely disciplined, exiled into remote provinces, deprived of their red robes (they were to be known as the Black Cardinals). But there was also a ray of auspicious light. At the wedding banquet Metternich, representing the Emperor of Austria, raised his glass "To the King of Rome!" This was the title that the Senate had adopted for the prospective imperial prince. It was reminiscent of the one borne by the heir apparent in the defunct Holy Roman Empire: King of the Romans. It seemed as though Austria, out of a millennial past, were acknowledging the supremacy of the new Charlemagne.

Marie-Louise was only nineteen; carefully educated —she could be insipid in five languages—she was wholly ignorant of the world beyond the rules of etiquette. She was devoid of that inner courtesy, that delicate, almost playful sympathy, which had been the key to Josephine's graciousness. She acted her part stiffly, correctly. She made no attempt to be a Marie-Antoinette: in politics, her influence was nil. But her very presence strengthened, if it did not create, certain tendencies within the Empire; and on the whole they were disastrous.

There is an aspect of Marie-Louise's influence that reputable scholars are strongly tempted to leave alone: its discussion might offend Victorian delicacy, and it is strictly incapable of proof. Marie-Louise, immature and innocent, turned out to be healthily sensual. The combination—*l'ingénue amoureuse*—had a piquancy that appealed to the forty-year-old veteran. A hero of legend, he was none the less a man. For months the supreme egotist had one guiding thought: to please his exacting young wife. He even attempted to learn dancing. Now, those months of conjugal dalliance were critical. He had to watch both the indecisive warfare in Spain and the growing menace in the East. The Napoleon of 1805 would have decided which problem to defer, which to liquidate; and by what means, force or negotiations. The Napoleon of 1810-11 remained in a haze. He knew the evils of hesitation, which had caused the downfall of Prussia; and now he, the master of energy, was among the drifters.

This paralysis of the will came with Marie-Louise; perhaps to some appreciable extent through Marie-Louise. It is far from certain that she should bear the sole, or even the chief, responsibility. Age offers a more obvious explanation. Napoleon was forty, and just reaching his prime. But he had lived with incredible intensity: some of his years were decades. We know what ravages a few years of war wrought on the physique, and perhaps even on the mental fibre, of Lincoln, Wilson, Roosevelt. And even if he had remained the alert young leader of 1796, at ease in battle, administration, diplomacy, his task by 1810 had grown complex beyond human control. He was to be his masterly self

again on the battlefield, in the German campaign of
1813, in the French Campaign of 1814; in politics and
diplomacy he was floundering. He had lost Talleyrand;
he was soon to discard Fouché: even when he did not
solicit their advice, the presence of these two men was
an intellectual challenge. Without them, he gravitated to
the level of a Champagny or a Savary.

The advent of Marie-Louise had another and more
obvious consequence: it coincided with, and accelerated,
a sharp reactionary trend in the régime. The change had
been gradual but irreversible. The ideal of the early
Consulate had been appeasement, fusion: but the Revolution was taken as a fact beyond dispute. The survivors
of the *ancien régime* were welcome in the new, provided they accepted its principles and achievements.
Such was, in particular, Fouché's attitude towards the
returning *émigrés*. By imperceptible steps, monarchical
forms were restored: even under the Consulate there was
something of a court, subjected to an increasingly rigid
etiquette. Old titles became assets. Nobles were preferred even in the officers' corps, hitherto overwhelm-
ingly plebeian, and even in the bureaucracy, once the
preserve of the middle class. Then an imperial nobility
was manufactured: a handful of princes, some three
dozen dukes, counts and barons by the score. A system
of entail (*majorats*) was intended to restore the right of
primogeniture among privileged families. From the
throne down to the local gentry, the hereditary principle
prevailed over Napoleon's great promise: irrespective
of origins, a free field for all talents.

Now the nobles no longer crept back individually,
chastened, accepting history: they were sought after. In
December 1809, in preparation for his Austrian marriage,
Napoleon "drafted" thirty men of high birth to serve as
his chamberlains ("Only those people know how to

serve"). Young noblemen were ordered into military schools so that the democratic taint might gradually be removed from the army.

The Empire of 1810 might indeed have been called "the Restoration". It was a Bourbon régime—with the Bourbons in exile. Napoleon himself was carried by this tide of reaction farther than he knew or desired. He was still attempting to preserve a balance. If he chose a Habsburg as his Empress, he believed that she would have to adapt herself to a court of revolutionary origin: "She will be playing whist with two regicides, Cambacérès and Fouché." But the logic of the situation was stronger than his middle-road intentions. Lebrun, once Third Consul, now Arch Treasurer, formulated the change with perfect clearness: to call to the French throne the great-niece of Marie-Antoinette was an act of repentance, an expiation. The Revolution was thereby sentenced. Napoleon, willy-nilly, accepted that view. He, the upstart of genius, became a legitimist. He referred to "my uncle Louis XVI" with apparent casualness. Now it was no longer the *émigrés*, but the regicides who were barely tolerated, and only if duly penitent. Cambacérès, shrewdest of time-servers, retained his ornamental positions. But Fouché had to go.

For Fouché's long-expected, ever-deferred disgrace, there was an obvious justification: he had been caught in surreptitious peace negotiations with England, in which King Louis of Holland had been innocently enmeshed. Those, however, who expected a sensational execution of the regicide, the former Terrorist, the butcher of Lyon, the unregenerate Jacobin, were disappointed. Napoleon's wrath spent itself in words. He staged one of his famous fits of towering rage (2 June, 1810). Fouché had to surrender his beloved Ministry of Police; but he remained Duke of Otranto and a Senator.

He was even made Governor of the Papal States; but he was ordered to yield certain documents, and, as he attempted to elude the request, his appointment to Rome was cancelled. He was sent, in dignified semi-exile, to his Senatorial seat at Aix. Napoleon took no further measures against him. Later, Eliza, now Grand Duchess of Tuscany, effected a show of reconciliation. In 1813 Fouché was made Governor of the Illyrian Provinces, an exposed outpost—indeed, a forlorn hope—where he showed competence and dignity.

The longanimity of Napoleon towards a man he so thoroughly distrusted is hard to explain. Fouché had been active on Napoleon's behalf in Brumaire; he had served admirably as the watchdog of the home front. But his manifest independence absolved Napoleon of any gratitude. It seems as though Napoleon himself were impressed by the "legend" of Fouché, the man from whom no secrets were hid. The greatest of these secrets may have been that Fouché, and Fouché alone, knew exactly the state of public opinion: a mystery the Emperor preferred not to probe.

Paradoxically, Fouché was regretted: not merely by the last Jacobins, who considered him as their shield, but by those aristocrats who, as early as 1800, had with some reluctance accepted Napoleon's rule. Fouché had dealt courteously with them, provided that they did not engage in conspiracies. The appointment of Savary as his successor created consternation; instead of a ripe statesman, a rough and witless soldier was to run the imperial police. Fouché, apparently resigned to his retirement, held himself in readiness to serve Napoleon again, but on his own terms; and if those terms were not met, to destroy him.

.   .   .   .   .

I

The situation in Spain and Portugal remained tragically confused. The masses and the clergy were passionately hostile to the invaders. But there were no more Baylens: in the field, the insurgents were no match for the French armies. Sir Arthur Wellesley, soon to be Viscount Wellington, was unable to make decisive gains. A precisian and a martinet, he was admirable in the handling of seasoned troops, but he had little use for the ubiquitous, disorderly, and heroic guerrilla fighters. He was not heartily supported by his own government: Spain was a heavy drain on the British treasury; the results, for many weary months, were not sensational; and the Cabinet grudged the cost. For two years Wellington, refraining from any lightning offensive, patiently watched the exhaustion and dissensions of the French.

Napoleon had large contingents in the Peninsula, with some of his most capable commanders. They should have been able, he thought, to drive Wellington out, as Sir John Moore had been driven, and at the same time to impose some kind of order upon the unhappy Kingdom. As a matter of fact, they almost did: there was a moment when only Cádiz and Lisbon were still holding out. Soult even inherited Junot's dream, and fancied himself for a while as King Nicholas of Portugal. The greatest weakness of the French besides their uneasy conscience was their lack of unity. For King Joseph and his military adviser Jourdan they had but scant respect. Most generals were thinking of booty first of all: Soult became notorious in this respect only for his lack of discretion.

Masséna was sent to take command. His pre-eminence among his peers should have been undisputed. He was the hero of Rivoli, the victor of Zurich, the stubborn defender of Genoa, the man who had saved the day at Aspern and clinched the victory at Wagram. But even Masséna was unable to curb the fractiousness of the

French high command. His subordinates excused themselves by declaring that "he had aged". Soult at one time, Ney at another, refused point-blank to obey his orders. Masséna pushed Wellington back to the lines of Torres Vedras, which protected Lisbon: a triple defence of massive earthworks, with redoubts at the critical points, impregnable except at heavy cost. Masséna sent messenger after messenger to Napoleon: only the Emperor's presence could restore discipline among the generals and revive the fighting spirit of the troops. Napoleon, now unsure of grasp and flabby of will, gave evasive answers.

In despair, his lines of communication insecure, Masséna decided to withdraw. At first, Wellington simply let famine and discouragement destroy his opponents: whole companies deserted, irreplaceable ammunition had to be abandoned. When Wellington struck at last, he found there was fire still in the old lion of Rivoli: had Bessières properly seconded Masséna, the Battle of Fuentes de Onoro (5 May, 1811) might have been a resounding French victory. As it was, Masséna was forced to retire as far as Salamanca. He was, rather unjustly, made responsible for the failure of the whole campaign and was never entrusted with high command again. The fiasco was undeniable, and its effect immense throughout Europe. Baylen might have been an accident; Masséna's withdrawal was a defeat of the first magnitude.

Napoleon's desire to cut his losses in Spain was intelligible enough. He seems to have considered the right solution: to wash his hands of the whole mess, restore Ferdinand VII, recall the two hundred thousand men he so badly needed against Russia. But he no longer had the sharpness of vision and the moral courage to make such a decision. His troops remained in Spain, weakened by constant drafts for other fronts, at the very

moment when they should have been either reinforced
or withdrawn.

While Masséna was effecting his disastrous retreat,
Napoleon's thoughts were absorbed by what seemed to
him a far more momentous event. The young Empress
was with child. On the evening of 19 March, 1811, she
suffered the first pains. Early the next morning Dubois,
the *accoucheur,* told the Emperor in consternation that
the delivery would be difficult. 'Save the mother,'
Napoleon said. The forceps had to be used; the great
Corvisart was called. At last, at a quarter to nine, the
child was born. For a few anxious moments the frail life
was uncertain. A faint little cry: the Emperor had an heir.

Cambacérès passed the word, and the guns started
their solemn boom. Twenty-one salvos for a girl, one
hundred and one for a boy. When the twenty-second
detonation was heard, Paris went wild. For good or evil,
Napoleon was still inseparable from France: the whole
capital rejoiced with the man and the ruler. It was one
of those instants of communion which are so rare in the
history of any nation. The 20th of March, 1811, appeared
to be the climax of the Empire. As in Victor Hugo's great
ode, the Master may have felt: "The future, the future,
the future is mine!"

This outburst of loyalty was sincere; it did not prove
lasting. The baptism of the King of Rome, on 9 June,
1811, was an anticlimax. Nothing more gorgeous could
be conceived. The procession was interminable and
magnificent. Robes of office, mantles and coronets, gold
braid and plumes vied in splendour. The imperial pair
appeared in full court dress, a crushing mass of velvet,
embroidered silk, and ermine, a glitter of diamonds and
proud diadems. Yet the crowd wondered in their hearts:
"Is this all?"

A last effort was made to restore the link between the new régime and its popular origin: the child was placed in the arms of old Kellermann, the veteran who at Valmy had won the first victory of the Revolution over absolutist Europe. But the Emperor himself remained aloof and stern. *Te Deum* and illuminations failed to revive the enthusiasm of 2 December, 1804. In spite of pageantry and fair weather, there was a chill in that balmy June evening. Perhaps the good people of Paris had been kept waiting too long while their dinners were spoiling. There were deeper causes for anguish. The news from Spain could not be concealed; the rumours of war with Russia could not be suppressed; the economic crisis was more patent than the gaudy frippery of troops and courtiers. All that magnificence was oppressive and somehow ominous. At what should have been the zenith of the Empire, there was a shadow of foreboding.

CHAPTER EIGHT

DOWNFALL

THE RUSSIAN CAMPAIGN, 1812

As the crow flies, there are fourteen hundred miles between Paris and Moscow, seven hundred and fifty between the Rhine and the Nieman. Distance enough to guarantee mutual safety. Not, however, when at either end there stands an autocrat, drunk with power and pride.

France and Russia had no quarrel; Napoleon and Alexander could not remain at peace. I shall list the grievances that led to the actual conflict. They were real enough, and of undeniable importance; yet not one of them was such as to justify the enormous cost and the fatal risk entailed by open hostilities. We should not sweep aside the facts, as Rousseau taught; but we should look behind the obvious facts. It was Bismarck the great realist who gave currency to the word *imponderables*: there are factors of a psychological nature that are more potent than steel and gold. Even a Soviet academician like Eugene Tarle could not make his book on *Napoleon's Invasion of Russia* an exercise in pure materialistic determinism.

We must not be afraid of the trite and the repetitious, for the romantic spirit is constantly alive within us, ready to transpose reality into a realm beyond or below hard facts and plain reason. For one hundred and fifty years

worshippers and detractors of Napoleon have agreed
upon the platitude that his ambition could brook no limit.
This is the sole cause of the Russian campaign, as it was
of the Spanish adventure. He wanted to impose his
solipsist delusion upon the universe: "The world is mine,
and the fullness thereof; I can do what I please with
my own." That there should be an independent power,
even a friendly one, was to him an insufferable affront.
This state of mind is *imperialism* in the simplest sense
of the term: the craving to command and to be obeyed
without demur, the refusal to discuss except from such a
position of strength that discussion will be a farce. Such
a state of mind is not uncommon; it exists, diffused and
confused, even among the peace-loving masses of the
most democratic countries. Stern patriots refuse to consider anything short of unconditional surrender—and
this applies to friends as well as to enemies. That
dementia imperialis ranges from coarsest "getting tough"
to the grandeur that was Rome: *Parcere subjectis et
debellare superbos. "Tout homme a dans son cœur Napoléon qui dort"* ("there is a Napoleon slumbering in every
man's heart"). Napoleon was unique only in the intensity
and absolute purity of that passion.

By 1812 the French had become immune to it. After
two decades of war they were sated with glory. Even in
1799 they had hailed Bonaparte only in the hope that
he would make peace. In the attack on Russia, Napoleon
was rigorously alone: diplomats, army leaders, administrators, business men, all advised against it. The common
people groaned; the veterans grumbled or conscripts
cursed; many took to the woods in despair. The whole
titanic drama was the inflexible and therefore insane will
of one man against the world.

Imperialism in this elementary sense—and in every
sense—existed in England. But there it was not con-

centrated in the person of an autocrat. And England
never had the power to coerce her satellites as Napoleon
did. Her one single-handed enterprise, at Walcheren, was
a fiasco. Even in Spain, Wellington would have been
powerless if the whole country had not been fanatically
anti-French. England had to work with and through
allies; so, compared with the French autocrat, she was
moderate, reasonable, civilized. She was not impervious
to the homely wisdom of "live and let live".

The case of Russia is more complex. In spite of violent
inner contrasts, England was a well-integrated com-
munity. In Russia, the peasant masses, the aristocracy,
the Czar, had not reached that degree of organic harmony
which creates a nation. The muzhiks were inert and
inarticulate; they had a vague horror of the Antichrist,
the godless French Revolution, whose flag Napoleon had
not discarded; and they nursed a hazy yet profound faith
in Holy Russia. The aristocrats were unevenly divided.
Superficially, most of them were Frenchified in manners
and speech; but the France which had won their cultural
allegiance was that of the *ancien régime*, the Paris salons
of the eighteenth century. The men whose "Enlightenment" had survived the shock of the Terror were a
dwindling minority; and even they did not allow their
liberal ideology to interfere with their class interests. Like
Catherine the Great, they were ready to agree with
Diderot on paper, for "paper suffers everything". But on
the realistic plane they had no thought of abolishing
serfdom.

The Czar was, and remains, an enigma. The mystery
of Napoleon's mind lies in its awful simplicity, which
was also the secret of its greatness. Alexander's mind, on
the contrary, was a chaos. He cannot be dismissed as a
weakling and a fool: compared with Charles IV and
Ferdinand VII of Spain, with George III and George IV

of England, with Frederick William III of Prussia, with Francis I of Austria, he was impressive in mental and moral stature. He was an autocrat like Napoleon, but an autocrat by the whim of fate, not through strength of will, a buckram majesty, a hollow man; he felt the difference and attempted to bridge it. He craved for prestige as intensely as Napoleon, so as to catch up with his own destiny.

He had come to the throne under tragic circumstances: his father, Czar Paul, had been murdered. Even if Alexander's complicity was not open or even fully conscious, still he accepted the benefits of the crime, and at the hands of the criminals. The shadow of guilt haunted him: he had to "make good" as an atonement. And his father's fate was a grim lesson: in old Russia as in old Turkey, despotism was tempered by assassination. He had to be a great czar, a slave, or a corpse. He knew that he had lost face by his inglorious flight after Austerlitz. He was conscious that, not the defeat at Friedland, but the alliance with the victor at Tilsit had been considered by many Russians an intolerable humiliation. He was thus swayed towards opposing Napoleon even though he was aware that resistance might mean catastrophe.

Alexander was a man of good will without steadfastness. His Swiss tutor, La Harpe, had shaped him into an enlightened despot; but he was too fluid to hold the shape. Yet his "liberalism" towards Poland, towards defeated France in 1814 and 1815, was not wholly unreal. He was to turn into a mystic, and Mme de Krüdener inspired him with the noble dream of the Holy Alliance. He was at all times a sentimentalist. He had a romantic bond with the royal pair of Prussia: had they not sworn eternal friendship on the tomb of Frederick the Great? He and they formed a most virtuous *ménage à trois,* the

charm of Queen Louise an excellent substitute for
political wisdom.

With the same lovable capacity for love, he fell at
Tilsit under the spell of Napoleon's personality. That
the monster could smile so winningly, that the fabulous
conqueror should seek the young Czar's friendship, struck
him as little short of a miracle. He was *subjugated*:
Napoleon chose to interpret the word in all its strictness.
But Alexander's Napoleonism, though very real, was an
infatuation, not a principle. A year later, at Erfurt, it
had already lost most of its virtue. Alexander was not
unprepared to heed Talleyrand's words of warning.

Napoleon called Alexander a decadent Byzantine,
sophisticated and shifty. But it was his own policy, not
the Czar's, that was tricky and unaccountable. On the
face of it, Tilsit should have meant a division of the
Continent: Alexander supreme in the east as Napoleon
was in the west, with a vague condominium over the
confused German world in between. But Napoleon could
not conceive of yielding an inch. He had created the
Grand Duchy of Warsaw; he swore that he had no intention of making it the nucleus of a revived Poland; then
he took back his promise and chose to keep Alexander
guessing. Poland, at that time as in the days of Pilsudski,
might have reached out for Lithuania, for White Russia,
for an indefinite share of the Ukraine. In Napoleon's hand
she would have constituted an instrument for containing
and rolling back Russia which Alexander could hardly
tolerate. Napoleon, against his promise, kept his troops
in Prussia—at Prussia's expense. Alexander, a mottled
soul, and generous in spots, deplored the continued
enslavement of his Potsdam friends. Besides, outposts of
the Grand Army right on the Russian border were far too
"neighbourly" for comfort. Napoleon dangled before his
friend's eyes prospects of vast expansion in the Balkans:

Moldavia and Wallachia were only a start; Constantinople itself was glimmering in the haze. But he was ready at a moment's notice to ally himself with the Turks or, given a chance, to seize Constantinople for himself. In the depths of his mind lurked the old dream: to strike at the root of England's wealth and power, to rival Alexander of Macedon by conquering India, with Russia as an auxiliary. Then, in bold anticipation of Sir Halford Mackinder, he would control the Heartland, and the World Island and the World.

In the campaign of 1809 Alexander, Napoleon's ally, took care to avoid any decisive action. His attitude was rather one of neutrality, and not obviously benevolent at that. He declined to give Napoleon the hand of his sister Anna: the courteous, evasive answer could not conceal the horror with which the proposal had been received in St. Petersburg. By 1810 the exalted friendship which had been "a boon of the gods" had turned into a cold war.

In January 1811 Napoleon annexed to his empire the northern coast of Germany, as far as the Hanseatic port of Lübeck. The Czar did not like to see the tricolour permanently waving on the Baltic. Among the territories thus ruthlessly confiscated was the Duchy of Oldenburg. Now, Alexander's sister Catherine was married to the heir of that duchy; the airy promise of some compensation for the dispossessed ruler sounded like an insult. In May 1811 Napoleon recalled his Ambassador in Russia, Caulaincourt. Caulaincourt was an upright man whom Napoleon had treated with a peculiar blend of high favour and cruelty. An aristocrat by birth, a liberal by temperament, he was a loyal servant of the Empire as the recognized government of France. But he believed that Napoleon's policy towards Russia was aggressive, and he boldly stood for conciliation. This, in the eyes of

Napoleon, made him almost a traitor. At the same time young Colonel Chernishev, as aide to the Russian Ambassador Kurakin, was enjoying great social favour in Paris, won the graces of Napoleon himself—and took advantage of his position to secure secret documents on the situation of the French army. He escaped in time; his French accomplice was guillotined; and the situation grew steadily darker.

All this, however, was happening beyond the boundaries of Russia and might not have roused public opinion to fever pitch. It was the Continental Blockade that made the Russians feel the full weight of the French yoke. In France and in central Europe, the blockade was a mitigated curse; it might even be turned into an effective protectionist policy. But Russia, with rudimentary industries, needed to exchange her natural products—grain, hides, lumber, flax, and hemp—for manufactured goods. The Russian ports carried on a fairly active trade under neutral flags. But Napoleon was aware that those alleged neutrals were Englishmen in thin disguise. He insisted that Russia enforce the blockade policy in all its rigour. This meant intolerable hardships for the Russians, at any rate for the most articulate classes, and in a cause that they felt was not their own. Napoleon's stringent orders seemed all the more galling when it was known that France herself granted (or sold) extensive licences to trade with the enemy. As the economic situation grew worse in Russia, the Czar imposed a high tariff on luxury imports such as silk and wine. It happened that these came mostly from France. So the economic front was bristling at the same moment as the diplomatic and the military.

Napoleon was tightening his alliances with reluctant Prussia, hesitant Austria, the subservient Confederacy of the Rhine, the vassal Grand Duchy of Warsaw; and

French troops, far from withdrawing from Prussia, were moving steadily eastward. Alexander, on his side, stopped the war with Turkey, sought an understanding with Bernadotte, now Crown Prince of Sweden, and erected vast fortifications on the Niemen.

In this tense situation the last provocation, as might have been expected, came from Napoleon. With the familiar complaint that the blockade was not properly enforced, Napoleon seized Swedish Pomerania. Alexander then sent an ultimatum demanding the withdrawal of the French troops and also the long-deferred evacuation of Prussia. This document was handed in by Kurakin on 25 April. Napoleon vented his anger on the trembling old diplomat: 'You are behaving like Prussia on the eve of Jena!' He raged, but gave no answer. With an autocrat, even the hint of an ultimatum means instant war. Yet Napoleon hesitated on the brink. From Spain came nought but ominous news: he wanted to write off the miserable affair, and could not make up his mind to yield on any point. French opinion was visibly nervous, almost openly restive. The elaborate network of German alliances was fragile. Even the great gambler shuddered at the magnitude of the gamble. Yet to discuss tamely with Alexander meant the total destruction of the legendary character he had been creating: the invincible conqueror whose word could not be gainsaid.

It must come to a trial of strength, then, the path of reasonableness being barred. Napoleon had not so completely lost touch with reality as to desire an all-out war. Two hopes remained. The first was bluff: to awe Alexander into submission by a display of overwhelming power. If that failed, there remained the chance of a swift decisive victory, another Austerlitz. To Caulaincourt's warnings and objurgations, he had in readiness the soldier's reply: 'One good battle will settle all that!'

It was part of his campaign, therefore, to show off his might so as not to use it. For days in May 1812 he held court at Dresden as Emperor of the West. The German princes rushed to his summons; they gave a splendid display of servility and even outshone their Erfurt performances. He had sent Narbonne to the Czar on a last-hope mission and waited at Dresden for the answer. Narbonne returned with empty hands—and empty pockets, for his papers had been stolen on the way. The Czar while professing his desire for peace, would not withdraw his ultimatum. The clash of wills was sharper than ever.

On May 29 Napoleon left Dresden. By way of Posen, Thorn, Danzig, Königsberg, he reached Wilkowiski (Vilkovishko), a small town a few miles from the Niemen. It was from there that he issued his proclamation to his troops: 'Soldiers! The second Polish war has begun; the first ended at Friedland and Tilsit. . . . Are we no longer the soldiers of Austerlitz? Russia places us between dishonour and war: can our choice be in doubt? We shall go forward; we shall cross the Niemen; we shall carry the war into Russia's territory.'

The army he thus addressed was the largest ever gathered in European history. The exact numbers are still in dispute: the estimates vary from four to six hundred thousand massed on the Nieman. In addition, there were garrisons, depots, observation corps throughout the vast empire and a large force desperately struggling in Spain. Altogether, Napoleon may have had 1,200,000 men in his forces; as many as Carnot had raised and organized in 1793. There was a radical difference, however; Napoleon's host no longer was a *French* army. On the Russian front barely one half of the soldiers were even nominally French; and included under that name were men from the recently annexed territories. The rest were Italians,

Poles, Germans, and even Spaniards generously lent by King Joseph. On the right flank Schwarzenberg led the Austrian contingent. On the left, the Prussians were incorporated with Marshal Macdonald's forces, which were to advance along the Baltic, through Mitau and Riga, in the direction of St. Petersburg.

Such was still the prestige of French arms that this unwieldy horde, without a common language or a common spirit, kept some kind of discipline for several months and fought with surprising valour. The Prussians, so soon to change sides, attacked their great friends the Russians with unexpected fierceness; they were nerved by the hope of conquering Kurland and Livonia, lands where the local aristocracy had been German for centuries, and was to remain German until recalled by Hitler. The Spaniards, of course, were hopeless in every sense. When a Spanish unit started sniping at its French officers, it was surrounded, disarmed, and every second man was shot. Napoleon was not cruel, but war is war.

For four days and nights the Grand Army, over four bridges, poured forth in mighty uninterrupted streams. The troops were in high spirit : it was the opening move in a fabulous game. For a moment, forebodings were stilled, discomforts cheerfully endured. Beyond the Niemen stretched mystery : a vast forest, dark and sullen; solitude and silence.

On 28 June Napoleon reached Vilna. Only four days before, Alexander had been there, gracing with his imperial presence a ball in his honour. He dispatched Balashov, his Minister of Police, to meet the French Emperor. The tenor of his message was studiously moderate; he even apologized for Kurakin's hastiness in demanding his passports. But the essential issue was clearer than ever : no negotiation so long as a single

French soldier stood on Russian soil. In plain terms Napoleon was requested to give up being Napoleon.

The Conqueror was still undecided. He spent nearly three weeks at Vilna, until 16 July. He created a provisional government for Lithuania: that is to say, he organized the squeezing of the country for the support of his troops. But he was careful not to turn his conquest over to the Poles, who were clamouring for it: for that would have made the breach with Alexander irremediable. At this late hour, Napoleon was still working on the hypothesis that the conflict which engaged one million men was merely a pique between friends. Let the Czar get rid of his evil counsellors, like that obnoxious Stein, a refugee from Prussia, and the allies of Tilsit would once again fall in each other's arms. Napoleon was magnanimously resolved to forgive everything; only Alexander would have to be more "loyal" in the future. Let him take example from those perfect allies, the kings of Bavaria and Saxony. Napoleon was merely waging "a war of reconciliation".

One thing he made plain: he was not leading a crusade of liberation, either for the oppressed nationalities or for the depressed classes. He was the Lord's Anointed, one—the first, of course—in the great family of legitimate sovereigns. He claimed later that delegations came to him urging him to free the serfs. The man who had attempted to restore slavery in Haiti was not likely to indulge in such democratic nonsense. He sent troops to put down peasant revolts in Poland. Only in St. Helena was he to rediscover himself as the Soldier of the Revolution.

On the Russian side, there were advocates of peace at any price; and some were found in the imperial family. But the determination not to surrender was overwhelming. The methods, however, were not so clear-cut, and the means at hand were very uncertain. The "Scythian plan" of luring the French to their destruction into the depths of Russia was not a deliberate policy. Rostopchin did tell the Czar (or claims he did): 'Your empire has two powerful defences: its vastness and its climate. The Emperor of Russia would be mighty in Moscow, terrible in Kazan, invincible in Tobolsk.' But no one thought of retiring to Tobolsk or even to Moscow. What the Russians felt intensely was the shame of allowing the invaders to desecrate Holy Russia, and the ruinous cost of a scorched-earth retreat; what they desired was a crushing victory right on the border. Failing this, their immediate object was to escape encirclement and annihilation. The Rostop-chin policy was forced upon them by Napoleon's initial superiority in numbers. They did not "trap" the French into Moscow any more than Joffre trapped the Germans into the Marne. Napoleon did not want to advance indefinitely, and the Russians did not want to retreat. But the crazy logic of the situation was stronger than their intentions.

There were good commanders on both sides, and moves deserving the stock epithet *masterly*. Yet the purely strategic aspect of this great campaign appears almost irrelevant. The objective was not to gain ground, but to break the opponent's will; and the will on either side was hardened by humiliating defeat as well as by elusive victory. The all-important factor was not epic massacre on the battlefield—Smolensk, Valutina-Gora, Borodino, were not decisive—but the humble problem of supplies. Not the climate, as Napoleon alleged in self-excuse. The army was decimated in scorching summer heat, grew anaemic in lovely autumn weather, and the intense winter cold after the Berezina only added a touch of horror to its death-throes. The army perished because horses and men could not be fed. An immense service

J

of supplies had been organized. But it was inadequate from the very first, to Napoleon's intense indignation. It could not keep up with the swiftly advancing troops; after the first rains it was bogged in the mire of primitive roads. The foraging parties had to push farther and farther to find a village not yet devoured. Oh, for the idyllic campaigns in Italy and Germany, when the armies were smaller, and the countryside richer, and some of the inhabitants friendly!

Russia had two main armies in the field; the principal one under Barclay de Tolly, a Livonian of Scottish origin, the lesser one under Bagration. The two commanders hated and despised each other. Alexander's presence with the troops, far from restoring unity, was a source of confusion. Russia's first victory was scored when the Czar was humbly petitioned to save the country from far in the rear. So the Russian defence was uncertain. A great fortified camp had been created at Drissa, on the advice of a Prussian theorist, Phüll; it would have been a deadly trap, and was abandoned just in time.

Although Napoleon had with him some of his best lieutenants—Davout, Ney, the dashing Murat, King of Naples—his over-all strategy failed from the start. He had hoped to annihilate first Bagration and then Barclay de Tolly: thanks to the ineptitude of King Jerome, Bagration managed to extricate himself, and even Davout could not retrieve the situation; Jerome had to slink back to Kassel. The Russians could be neither bluffed nor thrashed into surrender. At Vitebsk, which he reached on 28 July, Napoleon measured the abyss into which fate was luring him. He was incapable of taking counsel: still, he was impressed by the unanimous and desperate pleas of his closest associates. They were Bertheir, the ideal Chief of Staff; Duroc, Grand Marshal of the Palace, and a devoted personal friend; Daru, a competent administrator, in charge of supplies; Caulaincourt, whom he was compelled to respect. To their immense relief, he decided: 'Here we stop!' But this lapse into comparative sanity could not last. For a few days Napoleon was sullen and restless. Go into winter quarters in early August? Stop without a decision, checked, baffled, his Grand Army threatened with inglorious dissolution? On to Smolensk!

Barclay de Tolly, urged by Bagration and the other generals, made a stand at Smolensk behind antiquated walls. The first assault of the French failed (16 August). The Russians were finally dislodged from the flaming city; but they had lost only 6,000 men to Napoleon's 10,000, and they retreated unbroken. The same problem arose as at Vitebsk, but with more desperate urgency. It would be folly to go farther. This time it was Murat, old companion, brother-in-law, crowned head, who urged the Emperor to stop. He went down on his knees; and as Napoleon proved obdurate, he sought an exposed position, death the only alternative to disaster. His plea was not wholly unheeded. There was a moment of hope: the Emperor was heard to say: 'The campaign of 1812 is over.' Again his demon would not relent. 'We need one earth-shaking battle right at Moscow. It will astound the world. Let the timorous shake their heads: I am through with their advice. . . . Our very peril urges us on.' By that time the Grand Army had dwindled to less than one-half of its original strength.

So the mighty opponents "agreed to have a battle". Their honour demanded it. Russian opinion, or rather Russian sentiment, would have none of the Scythian strategy. The "masterly" withdrawals of Barclay de Tolly seemed to court and people, as they did to Bagration, the evidence of a craven spirit: Barclay was not a true Russian. The old hero Kutusov, no favourite with the Czar, was made commander-in-chief. He had been one

of the best lieutenants of the legendary Suvorov. To be
sure, he had shared in the Austerlitz disaster, but the
battle had been fought against his advice. Barclay de
Tolly loyally accepted to serve under him.

The momentous encounter took place on the banks of
the Moskva River, some sixty miles west of Moscow;
the Russians call it Borodino (7 September). It was fought
on either side with a savage valour unparalleled even at
Eylau. Not once but three times Napoleon was urged to
send the Guard into battle so as to clinch the wavering
victory. He, the man of swift unerring decisions, hesitated.
He could see that, without a stunning final blow, Borodino
would not be the Austerlitz he was craving for. But the
Guard was the backbone of the army, the one force kept
in perfect condition: he could not make up his mind to
venture it. The marshals resented his holding back the
last reserve, thus almost nullifying their heroic
endeavours.

As a result, Borodino was not even a Friedland, but
an Eylau, an Aspern. Napoleon called it "the hardest and
greatest feat of arms in the annals of the Gauls"; but
Kutusov announced it as a victory and won his marshal's
baton on that claim. He was boldly anticipating Tolstoy's
view of that fierce contest. In sober fact, Kutusov had to
retire, abandoning 45,000 dead, wounded, and prisoners
on the battlefield and leaving the road to Moscow open.
He still had an army unshaken in spirit, proud of having
shown its mettle, but so terribly mauled that it could not
stem the invaders' advance. But Borodino made it
palpable that Napoleon could not win. From Smolensk
on, perhaps even from Vitebsk, the Grand Army was a
huge wounded animal, staggering ahead on momentum.
In numbers, equipment, and spirit, its life energy was
oozing out at every step.

Kutusov's army marched sullenly through Moscow.

The bulk of the population went with the troops. A vast heart-rending exodus of a kind almost forgotten in civilized Europe: our own epoch, alas! was to see again such human masses driven like frightened sheep. On 12 September, at 2 p.m., Napoleon rode up to the Poklonnaya Hill: thence he could see the golden cupolas of Moscow glittering in the sun. The Guard, and the Emperor himself, broke into an exultant cry: 'Moscow!' Milan, Cairo, Vienna, Berlin, Madrid: how many capitals he had entered as a conqueror! But this culminating triumph was different. No delegation to meet the victor; no crowd, cheering or even sullen. A few foreigners, a few stragglers; streets and houses were dead.

That same night, before he had pushed on to the Kremlin, he was told that the centre of Moscow was ablaze. The fire raged for six days and nights. Most of the houses were of wood, the weather was dry, the winds fanned the flames, and no pumps were available. All that the French could do was to salvage some loot from the richer residences. The fire had been deliberately set: the soldiers caught a number of arsonists and shot them on the spot. It had been ordered by Governor Rostopchin. An equivocal personage, an aristocrat who spoke French at home and tried at the last moment to turn rabble-rouser in wretched colloquial Russian. Fond of dramatic phrases and poses, he had sworn: 'They shall not pass!' and left the city with the rest. Later he was to claim credit, then to deny the responsibility, for the deed. There may have been moments in which the hero and the histrion were almost fused in him. The grand and costly gesture, like most gestures, was futile. About one fourth of the houses escaped destruction: for nearly five weeks the soldiers found adequate quarters in the abandoned city. It was not lack of commodious billets that compelled the French to leave Moscow.

The "victor" wrote to the "conquered" a strangely gentle, almost sentimental letter: "I have conducted the war against Your Majesty without animosity. A line written to me before or after the last battle would have stopped my march, and I would gladly have forgone the advantage of entering Moscow. If anything of our old friendship remains, Your Majesty will take this letter in good part." To this touching effusion Alexander vouchsafed no reply.

The invaders settled down, wearily at first, then with mounting anguish, in the vast deserted city, gaunt with the charred corpses of six thousand buildings. For a few days Moscow was fairly well supplied: not a few peasants, indifferent to the clash of empires, brought their produce to market. But the army grabbed the goods and refused to pay, even in the forged currency that Napoleon had prepared; and the rustic carts appeared no more. In his enforced leisure, Napoleon made pretence that he was governing his huge empire as if he were at the Tuileries. The French National Theatre was long ruled by a decree dictated in Moscow.

Again, as at Vilna, Vitebsk, Smolensk, Napoleon was of several minds. He knew that he could neither chase Kutusov's army through the illimitable plains, nor march towards St. Petersburg, nor even organize winter quarters in Moscow. The obvious solution was to consider his raid on the old Russian capital purely as a punitive expedition and a solemn warning that he wanted to be friends with Alexander. This purpose achieved, he could with some show of dignity retire to a less exposed place with a better chance of feeding and recruiting his army. He waited week after week, when every hour told heavily against him. A brief cold snap was a stern reminder: 1807 had taught him the rigours of a northern winter. Prudence at last won a belated victory: on 20 October he left Moscow. As a farewell gesture, he ordered the Kremlin to be blown up; but the fuses were damp and the damage was not irreparable.

The retreat started well enough. The weather was crisp and pleasant; the sole difficulty was the abundance of loot. But, apart from a couple of serious engagements —Maloyaroslavetsz, Vyazma—and constant skirmishes, the same difficulties as in the advance harassed the return march. Horses and men could not be fed. The country had already been twice gnawed to the bone. Booty, equipment, ammunition, had to be dropped by the wayside. Even if there had been no Cossack patrols, no sharpshooters, no guerrillas, the army was disintegrating into a tattered mob. Four hundred thousand had crossed the Niemen: only one hundred thousand retired from Moscow.

At Dorogobuzh, Napoleon received ominous news. In the northern theatre, Wittgenstein was driving back Victor and Oudinot; on the southern flank, the Austrian comander Schwarzenberg, instead of holding his ground against Chichagov, had, perhaps deliberately, allowed him to pass. Strategically, this was a disaster: Chichagov might cut off his retreat. Diplomatically, it was worse still: it was proof that the Austrian alliance, mainstay of Napoleon's policy, was the frailest reed.

What affected him most deeply was a mere episode, already closed, but a symptom he could not ignore. In 1808 General Malet had already plotted against the Empire. He had been confined in a sanatorium: perhaps, like many daring souls, he was in fact half-demented. On 22 October, 1813, he escaped, donned a uniform, went to the Popincourt Barracks, announced the death of Napoleon, and showed a fake order from the Senate appointing him Governor of Paris. He liberated his former accomplices Lahorie and Guidal; the bold trio proceeded to arrest Savary, Duke of Rovigo, Fouché's clumsy successor, and Pasquier, Prefect of Police. All was going marvellously well until the conspirators struck General Hulin, hero of the Bastille, and "judge" of the Duke of Enghein. The tough veteran resisted; he was shot down, but his assistants disarmed Malet, and the farce was over. Slight as it was, the crazy plot revealed to Napoleon what Fouché had known since the days of Marengo: the whole fabric of his government would dissolve if it were not for the magic of a single name. It was then that he resolved to leave the army as soon as it was reasonably safe for him to do so, and dash for Paris.

At last Smolensk was reached, on 10 November. The staggering and famishing soldiers were hoping for a breathing spell and a square meal. But the city had been destroyed more thoroughly than Moscow; the supplies had been eaten up by Victor's troops; the Russians were in relentless pursuit; it was impossible to pause and reorganize. So the men had to slog away again, now in bitterest cold. Eugene and Davout were forced to fight their way through; Ney, at one time, was completely cut off. Miraculously, he reappeared: never had "the bravest of the brave" displayed more indomitable resourcefulness. But he rallied the main body with only a handful of men. At Orsha, the Grand Army mustered 24,000 soldiers in formation, with some 14,000 stragglers painfully following.

It looked as though Chichagov, Wittgenstein, and Kutusov might unite on the Berezina and capture the last shreds of the once mighty host, the Emperor himself a part of the booty. The crossing of the Berezina, with scenes of incredible confusion and suffering, lives in folklore as the culminating disaster. On the contrary, it was a last despairing victory. For Eblé and Chasseloup-Laubat, chiefs of engineers, managed to build two bridges on the icy river and rebuild them when they broke down. The troops crossed them in ranks to the sound of bugles and drums, an army still. Only the stragglers, who the day before had refused to move, rushed to the bridges in a belated stampede and were killed or captured by the Russians. Ney, in command of the rear guard, managed to hold off Kutusov's attacks. It was then that winter struck with deadly rigour. The thermometer fell to seventeen degrees below zero Fahrenheit. The plain was strewn with frozen corpses. At last, on 4 December, the army reached Smorgoni, a few miles short of Vilna.

It was a wonder that even a few should escape in formation, tortured but unsubdued, and their Emperor with them. A wonder of Russian ineptitude? Many thought so at the time and upbraided Kutusov for failing to deal the death-blow. His unwillingness to sacrifice Russian lives did not sound very convincing. Perhaps the old man was as his admirer Tolstoy describes him: sluggish, somnolent, and fatalistic. Perhaps, a Russian of the Russians, he thought too exclusively in Russian terms: the French were leaving and would never return: so why strain yourself in that devastated winter waste where the pursuers suffered hardly less than the pursued? Europe would have been spared three costly years of uncertainty and strife if the Cossacks who once surrounded Napoleon had managed to capture him.

The Emperor thought, or barely hoped, that it would be possible to make a stand at Vilna. At any rate, from there on there could be an orderly retreat. There would be regular supplies, and reinforcements would stiffen the shattered army. So at Smorgoni Napoleon felt he could leave his troops. In the peculiar logic of the imperial system, he was fully justified. Others could guide the tragic return. But Napoleon was France; he alone could hold the régime together, raise new levies, keep his allies

K

in line, create against Europe a still formidable front. The same thought explains the famous Twenty-ninth Bulletin, in which, frankly admitting the disaster ("An act of God; a victory of winter alone"), he calmly concluded: "Never has His Majesty been in better health." To the last, the single article of his creed was: 'I, myself, alone, and that suffices."

He had left the army in charge of Murat instead of the abler and more dependable Davout. But King Joachim had caught something of the Napoleonic virus. He, too, thought that his presence was indispensable in his threatened realm, and he abandoned the army in his turn. It was Eugene, self-sacrificing and modestly competent as was his wont, who brought the army back across the Niemen. The army? Berthier—Marshal Berthier, Chief of Staff, Prince of Neuchâtel—wrote in despair: "There is no army any more."

Meanwhile Napoleon was dashing along, with a small escort of Polish lancers. Through Vilna, Kovno, Warsaw, Posen, Dresden, Leipzig, Erfurt, he rushed unrecognized, Caulaincourt his constant companion. He poured forth a stream of memories, imprecations, and dreams, for he was none of your strong silent men; and Caulaincourt's notes on that tragic journey are to my mind the most fascinating of all Napoleonic documents. On 18 December, 1812, at night, an ordinary post-chaise deposited its fare, the Emperor of the French, at the Tuileries.

CHAPTER NINE

THE GERMAN AND
THE FRENCH CAMPAIGNS

1813—1814

So complete was the disaster in Russia that we feel it should have been followed by the immediate collapse of Napoleon's power. Yet it took fifteen months and the combined efforts of all Europe to force him into unconditional surrender.

There is no single solution to this great historical puzzle. The many causes overlapped and at times conflicted; and Bismarck's *imponderables* must be evoked once more. When the separate traditions, aspirations, selfish interests, and complicated intrigues of twenty states are thrown together, the result is a confused mass. The single will of one man at the head of a single highly organized system enjoys an enormous advantage.

Europe could not overcome all at once the tremendous momentum of French prestige. For two decades—nearly a generation—the French had lost not a few battles, but they had won every war. Not a treaty, from Basel in 1795 to Schönbrunn in 1809, that did not mark a new extension of their *imperium*. I have already stated that this long series of victories, from Valmy to Wagram, had not created, but had only enhanced the vast and complex glamour that surrounded France. Louis the Great, the French classics, the Paris salons, the *Encyclopedia*, the

155

Rights of Man, had their share in that incomparable treasure which Napoleon appropriated, coarsened, and squandered.

In material terms, it took time for the magnitude of the disaster to be fully realized. Napoleon could still boast that he had defeated the Russians in the field and captured their capital. Other countries could not rely on grim General Winter to destroy their enemy; and the logistic problems that had proved the undoing of the invaders were far more manageable in central Europe. Napoleon still held strategic positions: Stettin, Danzig, Torgau, Glogau, Küstrin, Magdeburg, Wittenburg, Hamburg, Erfurt, Marienburg. Most of these he kept, like the Nazis their "hedgehogs" and "pockets", until late in 1813; some until 1814. He had lost four hundred thousand men: but ruthlessness is an effective mask for diminished power. He wrote to Eugene: "Hold Berlin as long as you can. Make examples to preserve order. At the least insult from a Prussian village or city, have it burned down; even Berlin, if it does not behave properly." Bluff is a milder method, not to be despised. The Emperor ordered that "the Duke of Ragusa [Marshal Marmont] will pass through the city [Dresden] tomorrow at noon, his troops in parade uniform, taking his guns, and marching in the strictest order. He will send his baggage with everything that does not look well around by way of the pontoon bridge". The Napoleonic army was the finest show on earth, and the Imperator had to be something of an impresario. In the diplomatic field, as 1813 dawned, the whole of Germany—Austria, Prussia, the Confederacy of the Rhine—was nominally on Napoleon's side: York's surrender, to which we shall revert, might have been an isolated act of insubordination. Beyond their borders, the exhausted Russian troops would be powerless. Even Goethe was impressed: in his eyes, moreover, the stricken Titan was still invincible.

Napoleon was not doomed in advance except by the inner law of his being. If, early in 1813, he had *boldly* retired within the "natural frontiers" and allowed Europe to dispose freely of the vast spoils, the result would have been a fantastic scramble, during which France, an ironic spectator, would have had time to recuperate. Who knows? Napoleon might even have been called upon to arbitrate. This was to be the policy of Talleyrand at Vienna; carried out by Napoleon a year earlier, it would have saved the Rhine for France, and myriads of lives.

The inescapable fact is that Napoleon was Napoleon. To yield at any point was beyond his capacity: he must dictate. He believed—and posterity, not infallibly wise, has endorsed his belief—that his prestige was due entirely to his military glory, of which his conquests were the tangible signs; whereas it was as a peacemaker and as an administrator that he had established his power. If he abandoned Spain, Italy, Germany, and returned to the frontiers of 1795, he felt, his fabulous halo would pale, and with it his autocratic power at home. Freed from the incubus of war, France would have insisted on liberty, which to him was another word for disorder. He was well aware that the French were craving peace; so he had Maret read in the Senate a declaration of his pacific intentions. But in the same breath he asserted that "none of the countries joined by constitutional ties with the Empire could be the object of negotiations": this would have made it impossible to barter away even the Hanseatic cities or the Illyrian Provinces, which now belonged to the sacred soil of France. So Napoleon's concessions, grudging and belated, were even less sincere than the offers of the Allies. The Allies, being of many minds, might have muddled into moderation: Napoleon's mind was adamant.

The Russian armies were depleted and weary before they reached the Niemen. Many Muscovites, Kutusov among them, were doubtful about pushing farther. It was Prussia that struck the decisive blow. Prussia, after Jena, had been humbled, disarmed, dismembered, ransacked, oppressed more ruthlessly than any of Napoleon's other victims. And the wounds cut deeper, for Prussia had lived for fifty years on the glorious memories of Frederick the Great; her aristocracy was an officers' corps; her Queen embodied the proudest Prussian spirit. It was from Berlin that Fichte gave his rousing *Addresses to the German Nation*. The Rhinelander Stein had come to serve Prussia because, even in her humiliation, she was the last hope of a resurgent Germany. Hardenburg seconded him. The army had been drastically cut down by the victor. But Scharnhorst, Clausewitz, Gneisenau, gave it a new spirit and, through the training of large reserves, made it capable of rapid expansion. Early in 1813 Prussia, in her reduced state, was able to place as many soldiers at the front as enormous Russia.

The turning from grovelling ally to crusader of liberation came, not dramatically, but in a manner that was hesitant and almost furtive. In 1812 the Prussians, under the high command of Marshal Macdonald, fought on Napoleon's side; and, as we have seen, they fought hard. But the French and their auxiliaries were compelled to withdraw after failing to capture Riga. A Russian force managed to separate the Prussian contingent, now under York, from the main body. York desired ardently to go over to the Russians; but he had to consult the King; and the King instructed him, evasively, "to protect Prussian interests". Whereupon York signed an agreement with the Russians at Tauroggen (30 December, 1812) which opened to them the road to Königsberg. Frederick William III feigned indignation: a "beautiful soul", he could not dream of being disloyal to his liege lord Napoleon. The drab truth back of this shining virtue was that Eugene still occupied Berlin. An unwary French ambassador allowed the King to slip away to Breslau (22 January). It was not until 17 March that he struck a formal alliance with the Czar. Three days later he addressed a stirring appeal to his people and to his army. The great German campaign of 1813 had begun.

A lull of four months. A lull? Never, not even in Italy, had Napoleon been so formidably active. He was fighting for his glory alone, against the interests of Europe and of France; but the spectacle of that daimonic energy is awe-inspiring, like that of a great cataclysm. Vanished was the sluggishness that had weighed him down after he turned forty. One would forget that his short figure had grown fat, that his features, once as sharp as a newly minted medal, were now puffy and blurred. He was every inch the Imperator.

He won a last victory. Cajoling and browbeating (*commediante, tragediante,* as Alfred de Vigny would have it), he persuaded the Pope, now his prisoner at Fontainebleau, to sign a new Concordat far more favourable to Caesar. But the Pope, while yielding, reserved his final assent until he had consulted his Curia; and that last triumph of Napoleon, though it was celebrated with a *Te Deum,* proved illusive.

But his one great concern was to create a new army: for arms were still his *ultima ratio.* He had to call in anticipation the contingent of 1814, to recall discharged soldiers, to conscript many who so far had been exempted. The *bourgeoisie,* his mainstay, watched his efforts with misgivings. As we have seen, their most cherished privilege was that of buying themselves off from fighting,

and Napoleon was coming dangerously near taking it
away from them. Among the people, he could not and
would not rouse democratic patriotism of the 1792 brand:
that would have been akin to Jacobinism, the enemy he
had been attempting to crush for ten years. So there were
no volunteers flocking to the colours, eager to defend "the
nation in her peril": on the contrary, evasion and
desertion were rife. The proportion of new recruits to
veterans was larger than ever, and the conscripts were
sped untrained to the battlefield. Worst of all was the
spirit of discouragement among the officers, and especially
among the marshals. Napoleon did score one striking
success, which might have been symptomatic: Lazare
Carnot, the staunch Republican who had refused his
advances, rallied to him in this hour of need. He was
made Governor of Antwerp, a key position that he
defended admirably until the end of the war. On the other
hand, Bernadotte and Moreau had now joined his
enemies, and Murat, while he joined the Grand Army
again, kept negotiating with Austria in order to preserve
his throne.

In Germany, Stein, restored to office, was rousing
the new, still uncertain national sentiment against the
oppressor. Arndt, Körner, Rückert, Schenkendorf, Uhland,
with their impassioned addresses and poems, were far
more effective than the traditional diplomats. The German
princes, still hesitant, were requested by Russia and
Prussia to leave the Confederacy of the Rhine or take the
consequences. Mecklenburg was the first to secede. The
King of Saxony wavered with the tide of battle.

On 15 April Napoleon left Saint-Cloud for the front.
The first great encounter was at Lützen, on 2 May. The
French had a marked numerical superiority, and the
Allies, under the nominal command of Wittgenstein, were
loosely organized. It was a French victory, and in his

proclamation to his troops, Napoleon ranked it higher than Austerlitz, Jena, Friedland, Borodino. He spoke in terms that sound strangely modern: 'We will hurl these Tartars back into that fearful clime from which they must never sally forth again. Let them remain in their frozen steppes, the abode of slavery, barbarism, and corruption, where man is reduced to the level of the brute.' But the enemies had been pushed back, not shattered. Although Bautzen, on 20-21 May, was another sharp defeat for the Allies, it was not the "good battle" of Napoleon's dream.

The raw army had fought well, but it was in poor condition. There was cruel shortage of ammunition, and a disastrous lack of cavalry for reconnaissance work and sudden blows. Napoleon had to give up the hope of an immediate and triumphant military decision. He had to resort to diplomacy, not fully realizing that time was inexorably working against him. On 4 June an armistice was signed at Pläswitz.

This was the opportunity that Metternich had been awaiting. Austria, if she chose Napoleon's side, could keep the minor German princes in line. She had no trust in Russia or Prussia, and even less love for either. But she was in position to exact her price. Beyond mere rectification of boundaries, what she wanted was the complete withdrawal of the French from Germany and Italy. Austria would then be supreme in both areas, and the peer at least of France in the European field. To make such concessions while still undefeated seemed to Napoleon the height of absurdity. On 28 June, at Dresden, the French Emperor and the Austrian Chancellor had a nine-hour discussion, tête-à-tête, one of the stormiest, most dramatic, and most pregnant in history. We have to rely on Metternich's account, published long after the event, and manifestly touched up in his favour. Still, there are few documents in which Napoleon's voice reaches us so sharp and clear, commanding, angry, vulgar, and sublime, with odd half-sincere drops into familiarity and cordiality. 'My honour first, and then peace. You have no inkling of what goes on in a soldier's mind. A man like me cares nothing for a million lives. . . . If it costs me my throne, I'll bury the world under its ruins.' To this magnificent roaring, Metternich *may* have icily replied: 'Sire, you are lost.'

The armistice was to expire on 20 July; it was prolonged until 10 August. When hostilities were resumed, Napoleon had increased and tautened his forces; but now England, Russia, Prussia, Sweden, and Austria were united in a firm alliance. Bernadotte, head of the Northern army, and chief strategic adviser to the coalition, laid down an excellent rule: always yield ground whenever Napoleon himself is in command; strike hard at his lieutenants. This was a well-deserved tribute to the Emperor's genius; it was also dictated by the fact that the Master, naturally enough, always kept the best troops in his own hands. So Oudinot, Macdonald, Ney, were defeated piecemeal; while the stoutest of them all, Davout was holding Hamburg and could take no part in the main operations. Dresden was still a notable victory for the French. But it had a tragic epilogue: Vandamme, rushing to cut off the enemy's retreat, was captured with seven thousand men.

The French army was dwindling at an appalling rate. After so many marches and countermarches, the country-side was bare: bread and meat were not available. The unseasoned recruits, ill-fed and overworked, fell by the wayside. There were ninety thousand on the sick list. Numerical superiority was now heavily on the side of the Allies. Bavaria had already gone over to the coalition. The Saxons were to change sides in the course of the coming battle. Against 320,000 men, Napoleon had barely 160,000.

Blücher, Schwarzenberg and Bernadotte were closing in on Leipzig. The fighting raged for three days. Napoleon won his own victories: his defeats were "acts of God". This time, Providence—or improvidence?—denied him a proper supply of ammunition: 'Twenty thousand rounds, and I should have been master of the world!' He could not make up his mind to retreat in time. The premature blowing up of a bridge sacrificed the whole rear guard. Leipzig became known as the *Völkerschlacht*, the Battle of the Nations. It is commemorated by a huge monument of Wagnerian pseudo-barbarism. The German campaign was lost.

The French were in headlong retreat. The Bavarians, under Wrede, attempted to intercept them; but at Hanau the fleeing herd had momentum enough to push aside its former allies. Early in November, out of 300,000 men Napoleon had mustered in midsummer, 60,000 had reached Mainz. On the 7th, Napoleon contemplated the Rhine for the last time and hurried for Paris.

A brief pause. There were three armies on the eastern front, ready for the kill: the Northern, under Bernadotte; the "Silesian", under Blücher; the "Bohemian", under Schwarzenberg.

If he had had all the troops scattered in the German fortresses, and those which Eugene *might* have saved from Italy, and those that Suchet, an admirable soldier, was bringing back from Catalonia, Napoleon would have had enough solid veteran troops to stiffen his raw levies, those pathetic adolescents who were to be called the *Marie-Louises*. But all these elements of strength failed him: for many years the great realist had built on wishful thinking. Augereau, who was to operate independently in south-eastern France, never was a great strategist, and never fully loyal to Napoleon. Meanwhile, the south-west was morally lost. In October 1813 Wellington had crossed the Pyrenees; and Bordeaux was waiting for a chance to welcome the English and the Bourbons.

Meanwhile the Emperor liquidated—how belatedly! —his two worst mistakes: he sent the Pope back to Rome, Ferdinand VII to Madrid. With his assemblies he was as curt as ever. If the war was to be fought at all—and he refused to consider any other solution—the situation demanded a dictatorship. The Legislative Body had dared at last to raise its voice: Napoleon declared the session closed. On 1 January, 1814, he vented his indignation in a typical speech, colloquial, with sudden flashes of poetry. The pompous Roman mask is torn off; the man appears in his elemental fierceness: 'What is a throne? Four bits of gilt wood, a scrap of velvet? What makes the difference is the man who sits on it. . . . I picked up the crown in the gutter with my sword. . . . We must wash our dirty linen in the family. . . . You are but the representatives of local interests: in my hands alone rests the destiny of the nation.'

On 2 December Schwarzenberg had entered France from Basel and Geneva, in violation of Swiss neutrality. The main French defences thus turned, Blücher was able to cross the Rhine on 1 January, 1814, at Coblenz and near Mannheim. The two generals thus operated according to an over-all plan, but were independent in their respective zones, a situation fraught with difficulties. Schwarzenberg, in the grand Austrian tradition, was punctilious and slow. Old Blücher was impetuous: he was to be remembered as *Marschall Vorwärts*. This lack of perfect co-ordination gave Napoleon a series of chances: he could rush from Blücher to Schwarzenberg and inflict a sharp reverse on each. And he was on familar ground: his first success was scored at Brienne, the site of his old military school. Then came Champaubert, Montmirail, Château-Thierry, Vauchamp. At each of these sharp and fragile victories against adversaries who outnumbered him at least three to one, he ordered triumphal salvos to be fired at the Invalides: the Parisians shrugged their shoulders and the funds fell a few points. From the military point of view this short campaign has remained a classic: it rivals Napoleon's finest achievements in Italy. As sheer drama, this indomitable defiance of the great fighter at bay is magnificent, even though it was criminally futile: the aesthetic realm extends beyond the safe and sane.

There were diplomatic flutters, talk of an armistice, a shadowy and delusive congress at Châtillon. Caulaincourt, the advocate of conciliation, had been called in at last, but far too late, and with no power. The aim of the Allies was now clear: Napoleon must be removed. His heroic obstinacy doomed him: it was evident that he could never learn the ways of peaceful intercourse. And that aim was now within their grasp. Talleyrand, still Vice Grand Elector, sent word to the Allies: "You are crawling on crutches. Fly to Paris: you are awaited." Six years after Erfurt, Talleyrand's prophecy was fulfilled and his hour had come. The Sword was to yield to the Silk Stocking.

Checked at Laon and Craonne, Napoleon was planning a bold counter-offensive in the rear of the Allies, combined with an uprising of the peasants: a people's war. France might yet be the tomb of the invaders! He saw with amazement that his grand strategy was not countered, but simply ignored. In plainer terms, his bluff was called: while he was threatening to cut off their retreat, Schwarzenberg and Blücher were hastening towards Paris. Marmont and Mortier had fallen back to protect the capital. But their forces were inadequate, and they could not count on the spirit of the population. Throughout the country the French were going on strike. They refused to join the colours and to pay the taxes. Napoleon, especially after 1810, had appointed many royalists to administrative positions: these men could hardly be expected to nerve the population to resistance. Without a final battle, Napoleon was becoming an isolated adventurer in his own empire.

Leaving the army in Berthier's hands, he arrived at Fontainebleau on 31 March. He was still urging Marmont and Mortier to resist, were it only for a couple of days: in what despairing hope we cannot even surmise. But he learned that they had capitulated the day before, after a token resistance that was spirited enough at the Clichy Gate to win Marshal Moncey a statue. Marmont, a great favourite with Napoleon, had even gone over to the Allies. On 2 April the Senate voted that the Emperor be deposed. It justified its action with a full, damning, and woefully belated indictment of his aggressiveness and tyranny. Napoleon summoned his marshals to Fontaine-bleau for a last council: Ney, Lefebvre, Oudinot, Macdonald, Moncey, Berthier, with Maret, Caulaincourt, and the devoted Bertrand, Duroc's successor. All urged him to abdicate in favour of his son.

Senators and marshals have been accused of disloyalty and even of treason. If we accept the dogma that Napoleon was France and could do no wrong, the charge is justified. But there was no treason if they believed—and the fact was palpable—that Napoleon had become the sole obstacle to European peace. There was no disloyalty either: they were not, as is so constantly repeated, his creatures. On the contrary, the Senate still represented the Siéyès element, which had made Napoleon. Most of the marshals had won their spurs before Napoleon became absolute. They accepted their batons from him as the reward of their services, not as a personal favour. They had thought all the time that, in the common enterprise, the lion's share had been exorbitant; and now he was gambling away the fruit of their common efforts for the sake of his personal glory. The first allegiance of senators and marshals was to France, not to an upstart sovereign: it was Napoleon who had betrayed his trust. Their "crime" was not to have rebelled at last, but to have waited so long. At what moment is a man justified in turning against the established government of his country? There is no sure criterion: each historical crisis, each individual case, must be examined on its own merits.

Again Napoleon had waited too long: his abdication in favour of his son was spurned. Nothing would do but complete surrender. At last, on 12 April, he signed away that power which had become a shadow. The same night he tried to poison himself. That episode was long shrouded in doubts. The reports were contradictory, and the attempt was not consonant with Napoleon's invincible lust for life. Caulaincourt's testimony, however, is not open to challenge. A Catholic in name only, Napoleon had been brought up in the Roman tradition, which exalts heroic suicide: a great man remains to the last the sole arbiter of his fate. The poison turned traitor: Napoleon was merely sick. On the 13th he was again not merely resigned, but eager to live.

This bleak twilight of a glorious reign was prolonged almost beyond endurance. Napoleon had to wait at Fontainebleau for a whole week, until every detail of the settlement was properly ratified. That his treatment at the hands of the Allies was so mild—indeed, so generous—was due entirely to Alexander. The Czar had followed the armies; he enjoyed, not without cause, a unique prestige among the Allies and even among the

French. There were elements of chivalry in his strangely compounded nature. Prussia or the French royalists might have meted out to Napoleon the fate of Pius VII, of Toussaint l'Ouverture, of the Duke of Enghien. Instead of the dungeon or the firing squad, Napoleon was given an estate, the Island of Elba, with a princely income of two million francs per year. He was to retain his imperial title; he could keep a token guard and a miniature court: Caesar was given Sancho Panza's island to play with.

On 20 April, in the court of the White Horse at Fontainebleau, Napoleon bade farewell to a detachment of his Old Guard, kissing the flag and General Petit. No maudlin-ness in that pathetic scene: next to his own glory, the Guard was perhaps the thing he had most genuinely loved.

On his way to his derisory kingdom, he had to face the hostility of his whilom subjects. Lyon, Aix, shouted: 'Down with Napoleon!' Augereau issued an insulting proclamation. At Orgon, beyond Tarascon, he saw himself hanged in effigy, and a surging mob made him tremble for his life. For safety, he had to borrow the hat and cloak of the Austrian commissioner. At Fréjus he was courteously received with a royal salute of twenty-one guns by the English man-of-war that was to transport him. He boarded the ship, the *Undaunted*, on 28 April. On that very coast, only fifteen years before, he had landed from Egypt. On 3 May, after a stormy passage, he reached his Lilliputian empire.

Marie-Louise had been given the Duchy of Parma, and Metternich had committed her to the care of General Count von Neipperg. This dashing one-eyed hero and diplomat fulfilled his task to Marie-Louise's perfect satisfaction: after Napoleon's death they contracted a morganatic marriage and had three children. When Neipperg died, the Duchy was administered by a handsome if severe French aristocrat, Bombelles, who was duly promoted from major-domo to morganatic Prince Consort. The King of Rome, become Duke of Reichstadt, lived in Vienna with his doting grandfather. For Marie-Louise, her four years on the French throne were hardly even an unpleasant memory.

CHAPTER TEN

ELBA AND THE HUNDRED DAYS

1814—1815

THE return from Elba is the most spectacular episode in Napoleon's amazing career: one man, alone, reconquering an empire. Our purpose is not to belittle, but to understand. What kind of régime was it that Napoleon swept aside with such contemptuous ease: granite or pasteboard?

Napoleon's rule had lasted so long only because the dissatisfied could not agree on a substitute. A republic? But the name still evoked the Terror, and Thermidorian corruption; it was smeared with mire and blood. The Duke of Orléans? It was the solution to which Talleyrand and Lafayette were to rally in 1830: "a French Revolution of 1688". The prince, forty-one when Napoleon tottered, was shrewd, and tempered by adversity. But during the twenty years of his exile he had lived in isolation, at times in poverty. He had no organized party; he was profoundly unknown in France. A man fighting under a foreign flag, like Bernadotte? Preposterous! To give Napoleon an acceptable successor would have required long and laborious preparations. As early as 1808, Talleyrand felt convinced that Napoleon must be removed. But the chief characteristic of Talleyrand was his lazy opportunism. He was far-sighted, but not courageous enough to venture out and meet trouble. He was first of all an epicure: wine, women, and whist. His most memorable advice to his subordinates was: 'Above all, be not zealous.' So he drifted into Bourbonism because, although it was the worst possible solution, it was the only one that was ready-made.

The Bourbons had to be rediscovered. They were as forgotten as the Stuarts. Aimée de Coigny laughed in 1812 when a friend suggested a Bourbon restoration. Yet a few months later it was through her that Talleyrand came into contact with Vitrolles, the daring and pertinacious agent of the Pretender. In 1802 the ex-Bishop of Autun had reached a sort of winking peace with Rome. Now he received assurances that he would be *persona grata* with Louis XVIII. So he started preparing the way for a return of the Bourbons. But without zeal.

To prepare France for the Bourbons was the lesser half of the work: Chateaubriand, the only great writer of the age, was an effective propagandist.[1] It would have been wise to prepare the Bourbons for France. Louis XVIII, after his quarter of a century of exile and obscurity, was eager to return. Selfish and frivolous, he was no fool and no bigot. He had little desire to play the part of an autocrat. Approached in time, he would have accepted intelligent terms: a constitution frankly acknowledging the principles of 1789 and, as a symbol, the tricolour flag. As a matter of fact, these were the stipulations of the Imperial Senate when it deposed Napoleon and recalled the Bourbons—adding, with dignified effrontery, special guarantees for its own honours and emoluments. England and the Czar would

---

[1] In his essay *On Buonaparte and the Bourbons, and on the Necessity of Rallying to Our Legitimate Princes for the Happiness of France and of Europe,* written in October 1813, announced for publication on 3 March, 1814. "Worth an army of a hundred thousand men to the Princes." At least, Chateaubriand thought so.

undoubtedly have favoured such a moderate solution.
In the enthusiasm of the moment, the King's brother, the
Count of Artois, nodded approval to everything: 'Nothing
is changed in France: there is only one Frenchman the
more.'

But by that time the Bourbons, thoroughly undesired,
had become the only practicable solution. They need
not submit to terms. The King was surrounded by *émigrés*
whom their long years of impotence had narrowed,
warped, embittered. Of them it was said that they had
"learned nothing and forgotten nothing". So they rejected,
as Rousseauism and revolution, the idea of a contract
between sovereign and people. The King ruled by right
divine. He only consented to "bestow" a charter on his
subjects: a free gift of his grace, and freely revocable.
Eighteen-fourteen was "the nineteenth year of his reign":
the Revolution and the Empire were expunged from the
record. And as a sign of this uncompromising return to the
ancien régime, royal France tossed away the tricolour
that Louis XVI himself had accepted, and returned to the
white flag and the golden lilies. This disastrous turn could
have been averted with a modicum of foresight and
energy. Talleyrand refused to cross the bridge until he
came to it, but it turned out to be the wrong bridge.

In the diplomatic field, at any rate, the disowning,
not only of Napoleonic imperialism, but of the Revolution
and its great principles, had the anticipated result: the
treaty between the Allies and the restored French monarchy (Paris, 30 May, 1814) was remarkably mild. France
retained, not only her boundaries of 1792, but Avignon,
Savoy, and a few strongholds on the north-east frontier.
No war indemnity, while imperial France had exacted so
much. Even the works of art looted for twenty years
were not reclaimed. And the restored Bourbons resumed
at once their place in the councils of Europe, a place

second to none. Talleyrand represented Louis XVIII at the Congress of Vienna with unbowed head—indeed, with his familiar touch of princely insolence. After all, Louis was the only sovereign who had never made peace with Napoleon. As a balm to dynastic vanity, this policy was an incomparable achievement. The French people refused to take it seriously.

Unfortunately, because Talleyrand had been forced to accept the Bourbons on their claim of legitimacy, not on the basis of national consent, he was compelled to play the same card at Vienna, and the results were disastrous. He was right in abandoning without haggling all the fortified places still held by French troops: they were not genuine assets. He might have secured Belgium; and he might have installed some friendly sovereign like the King of Saxony on the Rhine, instead of the inimical and insatiable Prussians. In the confused Europe of 1814, now that sheer military adventure had been ruled out, three forces were at work: the national and democratic, still inchoate and frankly revolutionary; the *bourgeois* liberal, seen at its best in England; and the traditionalist, legitimist, or absolutist, represented by Austria. We may easily forgive Talleyrand for not anticipating Woodrow Wilson and his principle of self-determination; but if he had not capitulated to circumstances, he might have worked for genuine constitutional liberty, the Enlightenment without revolution. Instead, he constantly harped on legitimacy, in which he himself had no faith. Legitimacy fastened upon central Europe thirty years and more of the Metternich régime, as dull and heavy as lead. It gave his clients, the Bourbons, a temporary advantage, but it created a gulf between them and modern France. It must be noted that Talleyrand was soon to be discarded by the Bourbons, and that he turned against the régime he had done so much to create. His many apostasies are the signs of his repeated blunders.

It was not the Bourbons as men that France resented: it was *legitimacy*. As Napoleon had prophesied, when he disappeared there was a universal *Ouf!*—a sigh of immense relief. France would have been satisfied for a while with a humdrum government, but the white flag was a provocation. It made twenty-five momentous years of French history *illegitimate*; it definitely portended reaction without a check. Imponderables again: the acts of the monarchy were moderate enough. At its worst, the Restoration was more liberal than Napoleon at his best. But behind Napoleon there stood the principles of 1789, much as he had attempted to whittle them down. Behind Louis XVIII there loomed a clerico-feudal régime, Spanish rather than French, from which France had escaped with Henri IV two hundred years before. A phantom? But if you believe in it, what will strike more terror than a phantom?

Apart from this fundamental discord, there were many causes of discontent. The veterans were sent home with scant pay and less praise; from heroes they were turned into beggars and treated little better than bandits. Many officers with a splendid record were put on half-pay, while popinjays from the emigration filled the new Royal Guard. Peace had come, but the most objectionable taxes were not lightened. The end of the great blockade flooded the market with British goods: the industries built up under protection were threatened with bankruptcy. While the aristocracy—including Josephine—were entertaining the Allies, the masses, and even part of the *bourgeoisie*, looked upon the new régime with a contemptuous indifference tinged with dread.

All this is general history; but it is also an indispensable part of Napoleon's biography. A destiny is not sheer creation: it is energy moulded by circumstances. Obviously a lesser man—and a saner man—could not have taken advantage of the opportunity. On the other hand, even a stronger man would have been stopped at the first move, had Louis XVIII been a Henri IV, had not the whole Restoration been a senile ghost, at the same time frightening and impotent.

The Congress was dancing in Vienna when the news burst like the trump of doom: "HE has escaped!" Thereupon the assembled powers solemnly declared him an outlaw. No compromise: to maintain himself, he would have to defeat Europe single-handed.

For ten months Napoleon had been pretending to busy himself with his tiny domain. Pathetically, he had passed reviews and held court. More sensibly, he had explored every nook and cranny of the island and attended to the iron mines. His letters to Marie-Louise went unanswered; perhaps unopened.[1] But Marie Walewska came to visit him, with their little son. Mme Letizia, whom he revered, and Pauline, the irresponsible and seductive, whom he loved, joined him. His bruises were healing. His spirit—he was only forty-five—was soaring again.

He knew that the Fountainebleau settlement that had given him Elba was precarious. The French government—pardonably—refused to pay the pension that had been promised in its name. His guard was an expensive toy, and his funds were running low. The Allies had misgivings about his living so close to Italy, which was in ferment. They were considering a safer place of seclusion, and St. Helena was already mentioned. Above all, the Emperor received news from every visitor that the Restoration, imposed by the victors (this was not

[1] On 3 January, 1815 she sent him a curiously dutiful and coolly affectionate letter. It was the last.

quite the truth), had no inner strength. Now that the
foreign troops had been withdrawn, it would collapse
at a push. Napoleon remembered his return from Egypt
and took heart. This would be the most daring of his
gambles.

The watch over the island must have been extremely
lax. While the British Commissioner, Colonel Campbell,
was on a trip to Leghorn, Napoleon could do as he
pleased. Elba had a "navy", the brig *Inconstant*. A few
smaller craft, fishing smacks and ore-carriers, were
chartered or commandeered. On 26 February the
Emperor, with twelve hundred men, left Porto Ferraio.
On 1 March the diminutive armada reached the bight of
Juan, near Cannes. The landing was unopposed.

As soon as he trod French soil, Napoleon issued a
proclamation in his best martial vein: "Soldiers! We
were not defeated! Your general, called to the throne by
the voice of the people, is back among you. . . . Put on
the tricolour cockade: it was the one you wore
on our great days. . . . Victory will rush charging
ahead. The Eagle, bearing the national colours, will
fly from steeple to steeple until it rests on the towers
of Notre-Dame."

Napoleon avoided the obvious route, the valley of
the Rhône. His experience ten months before had been a
warning. And Masséna was in command at Marseille,
a determined soldier who had served him well, but who
had no love for him. So he went through the Alps, and
for days vanished in that grand and lovely wilderness.
The villagers, delighted with the excitement, came out
to meet him and marched for a while with his little
column. The test was Grenoble, the first city with a
garrison. General Marchand, in command, sent out a
battalion to arrest him. Never was Napoleon seen to
better advantage. He went alone ahead of his own troops,

opened his coat, and called out: 'Soldiers of the Fifth
Regiment! Do you recognize me? If anyone wants to kill
his Emperor, let him do so.' The royal officers gave the
order to fire; the soldiers rushed in a frenzy of devotion
to hail the risen demigod. Here the heroic and histrionic
blended to perfection. Napoleon loved to pose as a realist
and professed to despise all men: yet he could also
gamble on their chivalry. Young Colonel Labédoyère was
sent against him with the Seventh Regiment: he, too,
went over to his old chief, and five months later was to
pay for his defection with his life. Grenoble opened its
gates and illuminated its streets. General Marchand and
the royalist officers had fled.

To the government, basking in its "legitimacy" and
unaware of its own fragility, the enterprise, at first,
appeared preposterous. When, after Grenoble, the affair
appeared in a more serious light, the Bourbons did not
take instant flight. The royal princes, Artois, Angoulême,
Berry, went out to face the menace. The Duchess of
Angoulême, "the only man in the family", attempted to
hold Bordeaux. They were heartened by the support of
some of the most glorious among the marshals. Soult, who
thought he had drastically purged the army of dangerous
Napoleonic elements, declared: 'The man is an adventurer!' Ney vowed that he would bring him back to Paris
in an iron cage.

Meanwhile, on 10 March Napoleon had reached
Lyon. The response of the populace was enthusiastic and
at the same time ominous. What Napoleon could read
in the thunderous applause and on the vociferating,
passionate faces was not loyalty to him, but intense
hatred of the Restoration. It was the Revolution rising
up again, and Napoleon recoiled. We know that he hated
democracy, which he chose to confound with mob rule.
An aristocrat of sorts, and a soldier through and through,

he would never consent to be the Emperor of the Jacobins.

Three days later he resumed his march. Ney now had misgivings about that iron cage. He felt that his troops were wavering: in spite of Soult's efforts, there had been no total transfusion of royalism into the veins of the army. Ney received a message from Napoleon: "Come to me, and I shall embrace you as I did after the battle of the Moskva!" The marshal assembled his command, and gave the word: 'The cause of the Bourbons is lost forever!' And they shouted the logical answer: 'Long live the Emperor!' At Auxerre, Ney fell into Napoleon's arms.

With a chosen band, the Emperor hurried on to Paris. Then he left even those few behind, and went ahead almost alone in a post-chaise. He reached the capital on the evening of 20 March. All day the city had been tense with surmise. Thousands of horsemen, waving their sabres, formed an improvised escort. The six hundred officers and dignitaries who were waiting for him at the Tuileries received him with tears of joy. France had been granted a crowning miracle. As for Louis XVIII, he had ponderously skipped away twenty-four hours before.

For nearly one hundred days, wherever he went, Napoleon was hailed with delirious enthusiasm. Just beyond that pageantry of triumph he could feel the void and the cold: France was not with him. His terrible solipsism, his lonely pride, raised him above vanity: he alone could deceive himself, and this time he was not deceived. There were in him a madman, a poet, a supreme technician, and a morose realist. The realist had the last word: he said: 'They allowed me to return as they allowed the Bourbons to depart.' France had been reconquered in three weeks without a shot. But this most glorious of his campaigns was only a luminous, evanescent streak. The implacable reality was infinite weariness, scepticism, and gloom.

No more "legitimacy" for Napoleon. He could no longer pose as "the nephew of Louis XVI": Louis XVIII had spoiled that game for him. No democratic uprising either: the one constant note in his career was his refusal to be the Emperor of the Reds. His sole concession to democracy was the plebiscite: a question from on high: "Myself, or chaos"; no discussion; and a thundering assent: *Vox Populi*. As it was in the beginning of his power, so it remained to the very end: Napoleon had to seek support in the middle class, the Believers in Property. But he complained that Louis XVIII had spoiled his *bourgeoisie* for him. Pale, equivocal, vaguely threatening, the Restoration was none the less a constitutional government. Dissenting opinions could be voiced in the chambers and in the Press. The *bourgeoisie* had recovered their power of speech after ten years of imperial silence: they could not be hushed again. If Napoleon was to remain on the throne, it would have to be not as the victor of Austerlitz, but as an amended version of Louis XVIII—at least until he had won another Austerlitz.

The thought was highly distasteful, but he acknowledged the necessity. His solipsism was not unmitigated madness: he could bow to "the force of things". And boldly, since people wanted a liberal constitution, he went straight to the Mother of the Liberal Church, the Fifth Great Power, the indomitable bluestocking Mme de Staël—his pet aversion. He could not appeal to her directly. But he called on her disciple and more than friend Benjamin Constant. Constant had sworn a mighty oath that he would never have any truck with the tyrant. Now he and his friends worked on the desperate

hypothesis that the leopard could change his spots.
Constant produced a standard parliamentary constitution
with a strong British accent: two chambers, with
ministers responsible to them. This British pattern implied
a sovereign placed above politics—that is to say, above
action: a gilded figurehead. Napoleon winced at every
article: 'You are binding my hands. No one will recognize me in that garb.' But he yielded with his fingers
crossed. Give him his "one good battle", and how soon
would the constitution find its way into the scrapbasket!
As the only sop to his vanity, he insisted that the new
document, so flatly contradicting the spirit of his
previous reign, should be modestly called: *An
Additional Act to the Constitutions of the Empire.*

He gathered at once a surprisingly good team.
Caulaincourt, a good Frenchman, a good European, a
true liberal, ready to serve Napoleon loyally, was put in
charge of Foreign Affairs. His many virtues were of no
avail, for Europe held him incommunicado. Lazare Carnot
was entrusted with the Interior, a guarantee that the
Bourbon reaction would be checked and even reversed.
Davout was Minister of War. And there was another
star of the first magnitude, even though a baleful one:
Fouché. He was on hand when Napoleon returned. With
a mixture of fascination and loathing, Napoleon offered
him his old portfolio, the Police. And Fouché performed
his task well: the scattered uprisings in the west petered
out. Fouché had passed the word that it would be wiser
to wait.

The Chamber, elected by indirect suffrage, represented, as Napoleon thought it should, the notables, the
interests, the well-to-do. But they would no longer consent to have power snatched from them, as it had been
in 1800, when their leader Siéyès was shoved aside. They
watched Napoleon's conversion to liberalism with undis-

guised incredulity, and they were not slow to manifest their independence. Napoleon wanted his brother Lucien to be President of the Representatives: Lanjuinais was elected instead, with Lafayette as Vice-President. Both were committed to making the Constitution a reality. A plebiscite to ratify the new régime was ordered. The vast majority of the nation took no part in it. Whether the million and a half who took the trouble to vote were endorsing the liberal Constitution or the anti-liberal Emperor, history will never know. Everyone felt that all this was shadow-play. The one reality was the coming war.

It could not be averted: Napoleon's oaths of pacific intentions fell upon deaf ears. Fouché, more successful than Caulaincourt, did manage through his agent in Basel to establish contact with the enemy. His desire was to gauge realities: if there had been a chance of negotiating on behalf of Napoleon I, or at least of Napoleon II, he would have done so. Nothing would have suited his book so well as a regency of his own making, in which he would have had the substance of power. But Napoleon had men spying on his own police. He was informed of the transaction and roundly accused Fouché of treason: 'You are a traitor, Fouché! I ought to have you shot!' 'Sire,' the great police chief replied, 'I beg to disagree.' The same scene had occurred in 1810. Again Fouché kept his temper, his life, and his job.

A great ceremony had been planned to announce the results of the plebiscite. It was called the Field of May, a Carolingian reminiscence, but did not take place until June. It was held in the historic Champ-de-Mars, then a vast sandy waste. Napoleon appeared in a gorgeous court costume that struck a false note: the legendary green uniform, the plain hat with the penny cockade, would have been truer to the spirit of the hour.

For this was no idle pageant: it was a solemn vigil before the ordeal of war. The reading of the Constitution was boring: who cared for legal phrases? The thrill came when the troops passed in review and Napoleon gave them new eagles. He asked each unit to swear allegiance to the restored Empire; and they shouted back: 'We swear it!' Then they marched into the gathering night, after this supreme salute to Caesar.

Napoleon did not dare to order a *levée en masse*. He called for 700,000 men, including the soft and shaky National Guard. Davout managed to get him 400,000, of whom 200,000 were available for action, 125,000 ready for an immediate offensive. It was a far cry from Carnot's 1,200,000 in 1793, but it was far more than he had had in Italy. And it was a good army: conscription evasion had purged it of the less reliable element, and it had a large proportion of veterans. The command was the weak point. Of the marshals, only Soult and Ney, who had turned their coats as the Bourbons fell, were available. Mortier was willing, but sick. Davout was kept in Paris at the War Office. Grouchy, just made a Marshal, had the reputation of a good cavalry officer, but he had never commanded an independent corps.

The nearest enemy forces were in Belgium under the supreme command of Wellington. One army, composed of North German, Dutch, and British troops, was under Wellington's direct orders. The other army was Prussian, and led by Blücher. As usual, the Allies had failed to gauge Napoleon's rapidity: he was upon them before they had established close contact. Napoleon's plan was to destroy Blücher first, and he detached Ney to seize Quatre-Bras so as to hold off Wellington. But Ney, bewildered by his sudden conversions, had lost his nerve, and fumbled. The contest with Blücher took place at

Ligny on 16 June. The Prussians were routed; Wellington put it bluntly: they got "a damn'd good hiding". They lost 12,000 men; the old Marshal himself, thrown from his horse, was nearly killed. Had Ney secured Quatre-Bras in time and rallied to Napoleon, Ligny might have been another Jena-Auerstädt. Napoleon ordered Grouchy to pursue the fleeing army and complete its destruction. Then he turned to Wellington.

Wellington withdrew his troops from Quatre-Bras after a sharp encounter and took up position behind a ridge on Mont-Saint-Jean (Waterloo was his headquarters, far in the rear, and played no part in the battle). His one hope was to hold until Blücher could re-form and join him. It was a curiously elementary battle: Wellington, his lines once drawn, could not manœuvre, and Napoleon, in Henri Houssaye's terms, "distained to manœuvre". There was no intuition, no sudden grasping of a miraculous opportunity. Even his daimonic activity failed him at the supreme moment: before the battle, his generals were dismayed by his puffy, lardy face and lack-lustre eyes. Waterloo was a contest, not of skill, but of courage. Two brands, equally precious: the fury of the attack, the tenancity of the defence. Ney, in particular, in mental confusion and welling-up despair, repeatedly sent admirable troops to senseless destruction, and kept clamouring for more.

As the afternoon dragged on, it looked as though the slogging match would end in a costly French victory. But both armies knew that the decision would come from outside. Napoleon hoped that Grouchy and his 30,000 men, after scattering Blücher's troops, would rally the main forces in time for the kill. But the Prussians, under the temporary command of Gneisenau, were able to elude pursuit, reorganize, leave Grouchy wandering. They made straight for the main battle. Several detachments

reinforced Wellington in the course of the afternoon.
Finally Blücher himself, all bandaged up and, as he
ruefully said, "somewhat stinking", arrived just as a
desperate assault of the French had failed.

The news immediately spread through the fighting
lines; hope changed camps. Wellington ordered the
attack; the French resistance collapsed. After hours of
heroic tension, the sudden Gorgon face of disaster created
a panic. There are few such headlong routs in the annals
of France. Among the troops which, in square formation,
protected Napoleon's retreat, there was no disordered
flight, but a sombre, unbowed withdrawal. The Guard
fought well to the end, though Cambronne avers that he
used neither of the historic phrases ascribed to him.[1]
Grouchy, whose corps was intact, managed to rally some
of the stragglers. On the morrow of Waterloo, there still
was a French army.

There were many errors and many elements of chance
in his brief campaign. Things need not have happened
exactly in this fashion. So innumerable writers, Robert
Aron and H. A. L. Fisher among them, have wondered:
"What if Napoleon had won at Waterloo?" The answer
is plain: Waterloo would have come a few weeks later
and gone by another name. For Europe was roused and
united. One million men were on the march. The France
of 1793 might have met them, but the France of 1815 was
not with Napoleon.

On the 18th, Paris had been filled with rumours of a
great victory; on the 19th, official silence, and a rising
flood of anguish; on the 20th, the truth was known. On
the 21st, at eight in the morning, the now familiar post-
chaise brought Napoleon back to Paris.

What was to be done in this collapse of a world?

[1] "The Guard dies but never surrenders." "Merde."

Lucien, Carnot, Davout, an impressive trio, urged Napoleon to seize a Dictatorship of Public Salvation (here Public Safety would be too tame a term). He rejected their suggestion. Not that he had lost his nerve: he was full of energy still, even of bluster, and was neither penitent nor resigned. But now we find in him again the same co-existence, or rapid alternation, of mad gigantic dreams and sharpest realistic vision. In whose name would he seize power, the people's or his own? Pure Napoleonism, blind faith in the invincible hero, was a dead horse. And, we must repeat, he would not become the Messiah of the Mob: that would have been the negation of his whole career. Nothing could be done without the *bourgeoisie*; that is to say, without the Assemblies.

The Chambers made it plain that he would have to give up the throne. Two days were wasted in shilly-shallying, with some eloquence as a by-product. On the 23rd he signed his abdication in favour of his son. The Chambers ratified the act; there were cries, numerous and hearty enough, of *Long Live Napoleon II!* Yet all must have felt that these solemn and momentous decisions were meaningless. The Allies were far more determined against the Napoleonic dynasty than they had been in 1814; they were more powerful; they would have been more ruthless. But the Chambers, if they were not Napoleonist, were bitterly opposed to the Bourbons. They raised the frail obstacle of Napoleon II against the threat of the White reaction. In confusion and despair, they did not even follow the twisty logic of their own policy. They acclaimed Napoleon II, but they failed to proclaim him.

Realism is a word that stands for no single reality. As a rule it denotes selfishness and cowardice. But it can also mean the courage to follow plain common sense. Then its first axiom is: "Do not break your skull against

M

a stone wall." Napoleon was realistic in the best sense
of the term when he refused to seize a senseless dictatorship. The politicians were not: their thought was an
uneasy blur. Then Fouché took hold of the situation, and
posterity branded him a villain for his pains.

Historical condemnations are based upon might-have-
beens. A sober republic with Carnot, a constitutional
monarchy sponsored by Lafayette, a regency guided by
Fouché, would have been excellent solutions. But in
June 1815 they simply were not available. Retrospec-
tively, we may conceive of a Provisional Authority,
rejecting Napoleon, condemning his latest aggression,
requesting immediate peace, but at the same time main-
taining the right of the French people freely to choose
its own form of government. It did not happen. The only
decision arrived at was to maintain the Empire with
Napoleon II; and that decision would not stand against
the first blast of Prussian guns.

The problem was to have a government that the Allies
would recognize before Blücher reached Paris, and
Blücher was marching fast. Not that the Prussians were
barbarians—modern Huns, to revive William II's
unfortunate phrase. But the return from Elba had
caused among them a recrudesence of "Holy Wrath".
In that mood they might easily have yielded to the
temptation to give the incorrigible French a taste of
their own medicine. Remember that Napoleon, as a
farewell gesture, had attempted to blow up the Kremlin;
and that he had instructed Eugene to burn down
Berlin, if it did not behave. What if Paris "did not
behave"? The men who sang Luther's choral on the
battlefield of Waterloo might later, like Luther in the
Peasants' War, have shrieked: "Kill them all!" Wrath is
all the more terrible for being holy. Against this very
real, this now forgotten peril, the Bourbons, who had kept

in close touch with Wellington, were the only possible shield.[1]

Everyone felt, without acknowledging it, that Fouché was the man of the hour. In working for an unpalatable solution, not of his own choice, he was no doubt attempting to save his skin, his title, his wealth. This is not irrelevant, but it is secondary. He had to manœuvre, for the Chambers were committed to the impossible; and he manœuvred with his well-tried skill. He sent Lafayette on a diplomatic wild-goose chase: a congenial assignment for the Hero of Two Worlds. He managed to get himself instead of Carnot elected as Chairman of the Provisional Commission, which he deftly turned into a Provisional Government. His agents had never lost touch with the English and with Louis XVIII.

The immediate difficulty was the presence of Napoleon. To arrest him might have caused a revulsion of feelings, perhaps an insurrection or a military coup: some of the Napoleonists, having ventured all, were in a desperate mood. He must be urged to depart, with gentle but unrelenting insistence.

He had retired from the Élysée (his Tuileries days were over) to La Malmaison, where Josephine had died a year before. There fate granted him a few days of bitter-sweet repose. The young summer was perfect; the rose gardens were lovely beyond compare. La Malmaison had seen his honeymoon with power and glory in the magic early days of the Consulate. It was still fragrant with the memories of Josephine, who, in spite of all, had been his first, ardent, and enduring

---

1 History affords a miniature indication of the danger and of the remedy. Blücher, after entering Paris, was determined to blow up at least the Jena Bridge. Louis XVIII sent word: "Wait till I have reached the bridge; then you will blow me up with it." The bridge was saved.

love. 'Ah!' he told Hortense, 'how happy we could be if only they would allow us to live here!'

But General Becker, his appointed escort, was becoming urgent. Rumours were spread that Prussian patrols had reached the vicinity of La Malmaison. On 29 June Napoleon consented to move at last. His destination was Rochefort, a minor naval base between Nantes and Bordeaux, and like them a river port. In the neighbouring roadstead, two frigates were waiting, among the fastest in the French service. They were to take him to America. The party made good time; it reached Rochefort on 3 July. On the road, Napoleon was recognized, but neither insulted nor cheered. Joseph, who had joined him on the way, embarked at once with a few friends and sailed off unimpeded. On the same day, 3 July, His Majesty, Louis XVIII, the Unwanted, entered his good city of Paris "in the baggage train of the enemies".

Again a tantalizing vista of the Might-Have-Been! Imagine Napoleon, instead of Joseph, reaching the Western Hemisphere at the very moment when the Spanish colonies were shaking off their yoke! But Napoleon was still reluctant to go. For days he showed that fatalistic and fatal indecision which was as much part of his nature as his power of swift intuition and action. As in the Spanish affair, as in the Russian campaign, he saw the perils of procrastination, yet he could not make up his mind. He still vaguely hoped, without daring to hope, for a sudden twist of fate: a falling out among the Allies, an uprising of the French people. The one thing that reached him was a formal order for his arrest. The trap, half open ten days before, was closing inexorably. The British squadron patrolling the coast, aware of his presence, was fully alerted. His very last chance now was to escape in disguise on a small coastwise vessel. Napoleon could face any gamble, even the maddest, provided it was of a heroic nature, but not a gamble with the ridiculous. The fallen Titan could not be discovered sneaking among barrels: that farcical possibility was ruled out.

So, on 14 July, he determined at last to face the inevitable. He had moved to the small island of Aix. He penned a letter to the Prince Regent of England:

"Your Royal Highness: Exposed to the factions that divide my country, and to the enmity of the powers of Europe, I have closed my political career, and I come, like Themistocles, to claim hospitality at the hearth of the British people. I place myself under the protection of their laws, which I request from Your Royal Highness as the most powerful, the most constant, and the most generous of my foes."

A grand gesture: Alexander, who had a fine sense of sentiment and drama, would have played up to it. Posterity applauded that dignified exit. Again, the gesture was theatrical, but not histrionic. Napoleon was playing his part in all sincerity, with a touch of swagger like the heroes of Corneille. A gambler and a fighter, he was ready to shake hands as soon as the bout was over. Before we condemn the British for their icy lack of response, we should remember what the game, the fencing bout, had been. After ten years of aggression, Napoleon had been treated by his victors with great consideration; and he had broken loose to start on the same mad career again. This time no drunkard's promise would avail. France was to shoot Labédoyère and Ney for becoming his accomplices: the principal could hardly have expected leniency. And Murat, who staged a pitiful little return from Elba of his own, was summarily shot as a matter of course.

This surrender winds up the strange interlude known as the Hundred Days. Where glamour, not reason, is the guide, it seems incredibly mean to inquire into the cost. Napoleon himself once said: 'One can't make an omelet without breaking eggs.' When the omelete goes up in smoke, one may be pardoned for regretting the waste of eggs. Some fifty thousand lives blotted out or crippled; a harsher treaty lopping from France Savoy and a number of north-eastern places; an indemnity of seven hundred million francs; the Restoration more bitterly committed to reaction than ever—such was the bill, and it was not light. For that heavy price, France added a colourful episode to her chequered history, including the memory of the most complete rout in her long military annals.

The die was cast: on 15 July, Napoleon donned his uniform and had himself rowed over to the British man-of-war *Bellerophon*, Captain Maitland. He was taken to Torbay, then to Plymouth Sound, and transferred to H.M.S. *Northumberland*, under the command of Admiral Sir George Cockburn. The ship sailed on 8 August and reached St. Helena on 15 October. Napoleon's active career was over; his most astounding and most successful campaign was ahead.

CHAPTER ELEVEN

EPILOGUE

ST. HELENA, 1815—1821. PARIS, 1840

ST. HELENA is a small island, some forty-seven square miles of crags and vales, ten miles across at its widest. Lost in the solitude of the southern Atlantic, twelve hundred miles from the African coast, it belonged in 1815 to the East India Company and was much used as a port of call for fresh water, vegetables, and fruit. Steam navigation did away with the necessity of revictualling, and the population has greatly dwindled: from six thousand to barely three. It is neither the barren rock nor the green hell of popular imagination: the landscape is varied and attractive, the climate temperate and healthy. It may be that in Napoleon's time some poorly drained parts bred malaria.

After a short stay at the Briars, the home of a wealthy merchant, Napoleon was moved to Longwood, where he remained until his death. It was an unpretentious but acceptable abode: it had been built for the lieutenant-governor.

The material conditions of Napoleon's captivity—the number of rooms at his disposal, the retainers allowed him, the budget of his household, the range of his walks, rides, or drives—are of little importance. Most political or military prisoners, the field-marshals of the Third Reich for instance, would have considered Napoleon's lot an enviable one. The source of Napoleon's complaints is found in his letter to the Prince Regent: he had expected to be treated as an honoured guest, and found himself a distinguished prisoner. It was the plain fact of captivity that rankled.

So there was a minor St. Helena campaign directed against Perfidious Albion in the person of the Governor. Sir Hudson Lowe was an officer with a modest but creditable record. Oddly enough, he had commanded a brigade of Corsican Volunteers. Montholon, a member of Napoleon's little court, found Sir Hudson able, courteous, and not unfriendly. Still, he had been appointed as a jailer, not as a master of ceremonies. After the experience at Elba it was natural that some precautions be taken. Every one of these restrictive measures, however, reminded Napoleon that he was a captive. Then the British Government had never acknowledged the Empire. To Sir Hudson, his charge was officially General Bonaparte. Napoleon could not admit that the fabric of his dream had dissolved: "But I really *am* an Emperor!" Between the two men no social contact was possible: they negated each other's basic assumptions. They met five times only, each time with smouldering animosity. The representatives of France, Austria, and Russia would have been as "rude" as Sir Hudson: they kept out of trouble by never meeting the prisoner at all.

Napoleon won and lost this guerilla of pinpricks. He made his own lot harder: the officers of the *Northumberland* had proved that polite intercourse with the enemy was not impossible. But he had the satisfaction of creating the legend of Sir Hudson Lowe as a brutal tormentor clanking his keys and glaring at his victim with a Satanic sneer. The legend survives in popular tales and tinges even a few serious studies. On the other hand, Napoleon lowered his stature by engaging in peevish squabbles with a commonplace and conscientious official.

Napoleon's retinue was neither large, nor distinguished, nor congenial: no happy band of friends. The only one who was a natural choice was General Count Bertrand, an officer of engineers who had succeeded Duroc as Grand Marshal of the Palace, and who had inherited his devotion. General Count de Montholon, one of Napoleon's many chamberlains, had played no conspicuous part either in the army or at court. Both Bertrand and Montholon had their wives with them; both remained until the end. General Gourgaud, only thirty-two years old, one of Napoleon's aides, vain-glorious and irascible, was soon at loggerheads with the rest. He sulked even with Napoleon, and had to be humoured like a spoilt child. He left in 1818 after a duel, faked or real, with Montholon. The best was Las Cases, chamberlain, and secretary to the Council of State, a man of ability and culture, with exquisite manners. In 1816 a letter severely criticizing the Governor led to his arrest and deportation, as perhaps he had hoped it would. He was not allowed to return to France until after Napoleon's death.

Because of some misunderstanding at Rochefort the Emperor had with him no physician of his own. He attached to himself Dr. O'Meara, surgeon on the *Northumberland*. Sir Hudson Lowe found O'Meara something of a nuisance, and had him removed in 1818. After an interim his place was taken by Dr. Antommarchi, a young Corsican picked out by Mme Letizia and Cardinal Fesch. Napoleon had a very poor opinion of his abilities. Strangely enough, the second Constantine, the new Charlemagne, anointed by the Pope, had no chaplain in his little court. Finally Cardinal Fesch sent him, at the same time as Antommarchi, the aged Abbé Buonavita, who could not stay to the end, and Abbé Ange Vignali, who was described as "low-born and illiterate". But Vignali was a Corsican, and Uncle Fesch may have thought that Corsican blood was sufficient qualification for the care of bodies and the cure of souls. Like a true Corsican, Vignali was to perish in a vendetta.

Most of these men, and some of the servants too, were to write accounts of their St. Helena experiences. Antommarchi's is considered flagrantly mendacious, Gourgaud's thoroughly unreliable. The best by far is the *Memorial* compiled by Las Cases. The Master himself was dictating furiously—once fourteen hours at one stretch—between periods of apathy. He composed his Memoirs, Caesar-like, in the third person. They are something of a disappointment. Every reader is struck by the fact that Napoleon had surpreme gifts of style. He was a master of Roman eloquence, *à la Corneille*, preserved from ranting by the restraint of military brevity. He had flashes of imagination ranging from the familiar to the sublime. He was a master of pungent phrase: his description of Talleyrand is not easy to forget. The picture of a wreck in a storm (in a letter to Josephine, 21 July, 1804) is worthy of Chateaubriand: "My soul was in communion with Eternity, the Ocean and Night!" Yet Napoleon has never attained classic rank in French literature, as have his fellow general Choderlos de Laclos, his constitutional adviser Benjamin Constant, and a rather erratic minor officer in his Quartermaster Corps, Henri Beyle by name, who was to become Stendhal. The key to that disappointment is that every page of Napoleon's except his early letters to Josephine is sheer brazen propaganda. The man, who had undeniable elements of greatness, is obliterated by the immediate purpose. Among the innumerable writers on

the Napoleonic theme, Napoleon may well be the ablest:
he is far from the favourite.

But in his dictations and in his talks at St. Helena,
he did achieve his purpose, which was to recast for
posterity his own character and the nature of his reign.
It was a wheeling movement of incredible daring, his
strategic masterpiece, his most astounding victory—a
victory wrenched out of utter defeat. In 1815 he was
still posing as the champion of conservative order in
France and in Europe. He alone could protect Western
civilization from the double menace, the Cossack and
the Jacobin. He was still pleading with the other crowned
heads: "Do you not realize that I alone have curbed the
Revolution and saved you from the rebellion of the
masses?" And even in his first years in St. Helena his
attitude suffered little change. He still had some hope, if
not for himself, at any rate for his son. And he wanted the
throne of Napoleon II to be worth having.

Philippe Gonnard[1] has studied in a most thorough
and convincing manner the change that came over
Napoleon on the island. Material power was gone; the
dynasts among whom he had attempted to force his way
had cast him out. Even the *bourgeoisie* was forgetting
that he had been the faithful sword protecting the money-
bags. So he boldly went over to the people. He turned
himself into the apostle and the martyr of that democracy
he had so long despised. He did not call it a conversion:
he had never been wrong. It was the inner meaning of his
whole career that he was at last revealing: he had
admirably kept his secret. His democratic Napoleonism
is another *Additional Act:* there again he pretended that

1 Philippe Gonnard: *Les Origines de la légende napoléonienne:
L'Œuvre historique de Napoléon à Sainte-Hélène* (Paris, 1906). *The
Exile of St. Helena: The Last Phase in Fact and Fiction* (London
and Philadelphia, 1909).

there had been no change. The apparent contradiction between the old Napoleon and the new did not destroy their permanent unity.

The plea was plausible. After all, he had been something of a Jacobin in his early career, and *The Supper at Beaucaire*, which was radical enough, sounded sincere. He never had any faith in legitimist nonsense, though he toyed with it about 1810. He despised titles while scattering them like crumbs to the hungry. Above all, as a soldier, he loathed the profiteers whose buckler and shield he had been for fifteen years. At bottom he had kept in all things an ambivalent attitude: religion or free-thought, monarchy or republic, the common people or the moneyed interests, what did it matter to him as long as he had power, and power absolute? His sole enemies, man, class, or nation, were those who refused to bow down. *Debellare superbos.*

Napoleonism was a genuine religion with him—that religion of which Victor Hugo vowed to be the priest. So his solipsism assumed forms that must sound crazy to the free-thinker, blasphemous to the Christian: *Sum qui sum*, "I am the way". He spoke without strain in Messianic terms. He was the Man, the Man who stood for the whole people and for all peoples, the supreme incarnation of our common humanity. He alone could have redeemed mankind, so long held in bondage by the oligarchs. The oligarchs were crucifying him, but he would rise again in the spirit and confound them. And the oligarchs were giving him a splendid chance: after rejecting him, they had double-crossed their peoples. As in many campaigns he had hurled his battalions against the weak point of his enemies, the spot where they had failed to establish or maintain contact, so he now directed the massive columns of his propaganda against the point where dynasties and national sentiment had drifted apart. This masterly move was prophetic: when Napoleon was dictating to Gourgaud and Montholon, the bitter feud between the Holy Alliance and democratic aspirations was not yet evident. There was a brief flare-up of liberalism and nationalism just at the moment of Napoleon's death: but the great popular storm did not come full-blast until 1830.

Napoleon was forty-six when he reached St. Helena. But the tension of twenty incredible years had sapped a constitution that perhaps never was robust. In the leisure of his captivity, when it was no longer necessary to assure the world that "Never has His Majesty been in better health", he indulged in almost every kind of disease: according to O'Meara's report in 1818, "indigestion, catarrh, headache, rheumatism, swollen legs, inflamed gums, biliousness, and constipation". He had no good doctor at hand: he long refused the services of the British medical men on Sir Hudson's staff. Even if his advisers had been as good as Corsivart, he would have spurned their suggestions, partly out of fatalism, partly out of wilfulness. A doctor is a dictator, and Napoleon was unable to brook any authority.

The medical record of his six years in St. Helena is uneven and confusing: Raoul Brice, a French army surgeon with the rank of lieutenant-general, managed to make that confusion worse confounded.[1] The patient had moments of tolerable and rather torpid well-being, none of sparkling health and vigour: his mental activity, which was intense, appears all the more creditable. His principal disease was not properly diagnosed: there were squabbles between Antommarchi and the British surgeons. The one certain fact is that he was afflicted with a variety of

1 Raoul Brice: *The Riddle of Napoleon* (New York, 1937).

diseases which his physicians failed to recognize in time, let alone cure or even alleviate. In the spring of 1821 he felt that the end was near, and he worked feverishly on his elaborate Testament. On 3 May he received the Last Sacrament. Early in the morning of 5 May he made unintelligible sounds, which Montholon, with the ears of faith, interpreted as *"France . . . armée . . . tête d'armée . . . Joséphine. . . ."* He expired the same evening before six o'clock.

The autopsy failed to clear up the ambiguity that clouded his last battle with disease. Dr. Arnott, appointed by the Governor, gave the cause of death as cancer of the stomach in an advanced stage: it was the disease that had carried off Carlo Buonaparte and was to kill Pauline. The Napoleonists claimed there were only ulcers of the stomach, with adhesions and perforations; the deeper trouble was with the liver, and had been induced by the deadly climate of St. Helena: thus England had slowly tortured her victim to death. The British maintained that the liver, though large (or enlarged?), was perfectly sound.

The Emperor's body was clothed with the uniform of the Mounted Chasseurs of the Guard. A first coffin of zinc was sealed and enclosed in one of mahogany. This was enclosed in its turn in a sealed leaden coffin, and the whole in an outer box of mahogany. The work was well done, without embalming: when the body was exhumed in 1840, the Emperor's features were recognizable. The burial took place at Hutsgate, near Longwood, a spot he had loved and had himself selected. England was bound to deny him imperial honours, but she granted him the highest accorded to British army officers. The little colony soon scattered, and Napoleon remained alone in a grave that needed no name.

On 5 May, 1821, Napoleon was very dead indeed. Talleyrand could say, when apprised: 'An event? Hardly. Just an item of news.' But a great life does not end with death.

There was at that time little trace of Napoleonic sentiment: imagination loved to dwell on the remote and storied past. Sir Walter Scott found avid readers. Chateaubriand was the monarch of French literature; and after his example the rising romantic generation— Lamartine, Vigny, the "sublime child" Hugo—were ardent Catholics and royalists. They strove to view the Bourbons in a magic medieval light. This orgy of antiquarianism culminated in the sedulous will-to-make-believe of Charles X's coronation in 1825. Even the phial of Holy Chrism was miraculously found again. The Voltairians tittered.

The turning-point came just after that elaborate pageantry. Public opinion was aflame with enthusiasm for the cause of Greek independence: that the great Lord Byron had espoused it gave it an irresistible halo. Chateaubriand quarrelled with his masters. Romanticism evolved swiftly from an aristocratic mood, enamoured of the past, to a faith in the divine right of the people. And as it so moved, it discovered the figure of Napoleon. Not the Sword of Thermidor, not the martinet, not the efficiency manager, not even the conqueror, but the latest avatar, the Napoleon of St. Helena, the Prometheus of Democracy.

As against the dusty and senile Bourbons he was as vivid as a flame. By 1830, as against the shrewd profiteers of the *bourgeois* monarchy he offered an escape into a world of epic glory. So the Napoleon of the 1830's became one of the gigantic myths of the time. He assumed his place in that teeming Pantheon by the side of Prometheus, Don Juan, Faust; and he possessed very much the same kind of reality. A myth is far more dynamic than plodding common sense; it opens infinite vistas which, even though delusive, have a deeper appeal than a blank wall encircling a neat vegetable garden. So long as you are willing to suspend disbelief, the magic preserves its glow.

There were ten full years (1830-40) of militant Napoleon-worship. The craze was rife especially among *bourgeois* writers; Thiers, Balzac, Hugo, Béranger. The aristocrats—Chateaubriand, Lamartine, Vigny—held aloof: what they saw in the Napoleonic saga was the exaltation of brute force. A true man of the people like Michelet could not be deceived; the Parisian masses, profoundly democratic, resented Caesarism as a travesty of their ideal. But the craze continued to spread: on every stage in Paris there was a Napoleon strutting proudly, striking attitudes, mouthing historic words. The Vendôme Column became a place of pilgrimage. The Arc de Triomphe was completed to his glory.

This tumultuous movement I have attempted to study in my *Reflections on the Napoleonic Legend.* It was Napoleon's second life, far more poetic than the first. In the minds of most readers, and even of many well-qualified scholars, it has substituted itself for the chequered earthly career that ended in 1821. Historians even today piously accept the essence of the Legend—the epic sweep, the miraculous achievements, the apocalyptic catastrophe, the ultimate Golgotha. They do not challenge the saga of the Hero, the Genius, the Titan, the Demigod: all they do is investigate details which, however damaging, do not affect the total impression. Theirs is a glowing Fundamentalism, so deep-seated that the results of dispassionate research are never allowed to interfere with the Faith. If we seek *biography*, not hagiography, the story of a great life as it was actually lived, if we strive to understand Napoleon the human being, then we must bear in mind that Napoleon the Demigod was conceived in St. Helena, came of age in 1830, and was solemnly canonized in 1840.

For reasons of its own, the *bourgeois* government of Louis-Philippe deliberately adopted and fostered the Legend: it shed reflected glory on that stodgy régime. In 1840 the remains, poetically termed the Ashes, of the Emperor were brought back from St. Helena by the son of Louis-Philippe, the Sailor Prince, Joinville. The ship was called *La Belle Poule*, the Beautiful Hen. Transferred to a barge, the bier went up the Seine as far as Courbevoie. Thence it was carried on an ornate chariot along the great avenue which, under various names, leads to the Place de la Concorde. It was 15 December, "a day as dazzling as glory, as cold as the tomb". Hundreds of thousands thronged the long route of the procession. Canvas and cardboard monuments everywhere; banners fluttering; crippled veterans in their historic uniforms; martial music; tolling of bells; booming of guns. The catafalque, a shrine on wheels, a car of Juggernaut, proceeded with majestic slowness amid shouts and tears.

At Les Invalides the King, in the name of France, received the sacred relics from his son the Sailor Prince. A Presence filled the church and struck every heart with awe. And now, under the marvellous gilded dome shaped like a spiked helmet, Napoleon reposes in his tomb of red porphyry "on the banks of the Seine, among those French people he had loved so well".

N

NOTE ON SOURCES

IT is commonly accepted that no man in history has been the subject of so much writing as Napoleon I. It has even been asserted, more dubiously, that Napoleon fascinates the German reader more than Barbarossa, Frederick the Great, or Bismarck; the English reader more than Elizabeth, Cromwell, Marlborough, Chatham, or Wellington; the Russian reader more than Ivan the Terrible, Peter the Great, or Catherine II; the American reader more than Washington, Jefferson, Jackson, and perhaps even Lincoln. Napoleon is not in the same class as other world heroes in modern history: he alone belongs to the fields of scholarship, epic, romance, legend, and contemporary politics: for all modern dictators have a Napoleonic complex. F. M. Kircheisen attempted an exhaustive bibliography of the subject: *Bibliographie des napoleonischen Zeitalters* (Berlin 1902); *Bibliographie du Temps de Napoléon comprenant l'histoire des Etats-Unis* (Paris, 1908-12). It reached one hundred thousand titles. It was not completed, and for the last half-century the flood has swept on. It shows some signs of slackening, owing to World War II and its aftermath. Hitler has not displaced Napoleon in popularity, but certain resemblances are too obvious for comfort (Hitler's *imperium* was far more extensive than Napoleon's). And the atomic age has at last relegated Napoleonic warfare to ancient history.

I. BACKGROUND WORKS

If we desire to escape dithyramb, satire, and romance, the first step is to place Napoleon in his historical setting by consulting general books on the whole period. They are as a rule parts of series intended for the student as well as for the general reader. They are provided with bibliographical aids. Among the best-known and most easily available may be mentioned:

Lavisse *et* Rambaud, editors: *Histoire Générale du 4ème Siècle à nos jours,* Vol. IX, *Napoléon.* (I have been using the third revised edition, Paris, 1925.)

The Cambridge Modern History, Vol. IX, *Napoleon* (1906). (The later popular editions omit the bibliographies.) In these two great collective works, the separate chapters are by different authors; the general impression is therefore slightly blurred—as perhaps it should be. Ernest Lavisse, editor: *Histoire de la France Contemporaine.* Vol. III. G. Pariset: *Le Consulat et l'Empire* (Paris, 1921). William L. Langer, editor: *The Rise of Modern Europe.* Geoffrey Bruun: *Europe and the French Imperium* (New York, 1938). The preceding and following volumes in the same series have some bearing on the Napoleonic theme. Crane Brinton: *A Decade of Revolution* (New York, 1934); and Frederick B. Artz: *Reaction and Revolution* (New York, 1934). L. Halphen *et* Ph. Sagnac: *Peuples et Civilisations,* Vol. IX. Georges Lefebvre: *Napoléon* (Paris, 1935). (The richest in facts and thoughts; indeed, a masterly piece of work. But, intended as a guide for the professional student, it may be found too highly condensed for the general reader).

II. GENERAL WORKS ON NAPOLEON

They are innumerable, and many have achieved a high reputation. In many respects, Adolphe Thiers's will never be surpassed. Among the best-known: A. Fournier (Viennese): *Napoleon I*, edited by E. G. Bourne (New York, 1903); Holland Rose; William Milligan Sloane; of recent years, Fletcher Pratt, very lively, and notable for a clear presentation of military events. The most practical one-volume history is F. M. Kircheisen: *Napoleon* (London, 1931); a condensation of his enormous labour in that field. Emil Ludwig: *Napoleon* (London, 1926), remains the most readable. Ludwig acknowledges the aid he received from Kircheisen, Driault, and Pariset, all three excellent guides; as well as from Wildhagen, for whom I could not vouch.

The most ambitious modern work about Napoleon is that of Louis Madelin, the Thiers of our days. He did some excellent research work (*Fouché; La Rome de Napoléon*). In his more general books, in spite of his extreme bias, Napoleonic and nationalistic, and of his old-fashioned academic eloquence, he remains well informed as well as lucid. His *Histoire du Consulat et de l'Empire* comprises twelve substantial volumes. At the end of each there are very full *Notes et Références*. As a sort of pilot work, he also published in Fr. Funck-Brentano's *L'Histoire de France Racontée à Tous* two volumes on *The Consulate and the Empire* (New York, 1934-6). There are notes on Sources and Bibliography at the end of each chapter.

Hubert B. Richardson: *A Dictionary of Napoleon and His Times* (London, 1920), was very well conceived, and a revised version would be greatly welcome.

III. ORIGINAL SOURCES

The most essential is Napoleon's *Correspondence,* edited in magnificent form, but with unfortunate excisions, under the Second Empire. Numerous additions and corrections have been made since that monument was completed. It is too bulky and all-embracing to be of use to the general reader; but J. M. Thompson has given an excellent selection and translation of three hundred typical letters: *Letters of Napoleon* (Oxford, 1934). Napoleon's *Letters to Josephine* were published separately in an English edition (London, 1901). Also those, more sedate, to Marie-Louise (London, 1937).

The second great source is the St. Helena literature. The best is: E. Las Cases: *Mémorial de Sainte-Hélène* (1823), often republished and translated, in full or in abridgement; and *Mémoires pour Servir à l'Histoire de France sous Napoléon,* dictated by the Emperor himself to Generals Gourgaud and Montholon. These can be used only with the greatest caution, and are too bulky for the general reader. Many writers have been tempted to offer "autobiographies" of Napoleon, combining the St Helena literature with fragments from letters, proclamations, speeches, conversations. Among them: R. M. Johnston: *The Corsican: A Diary of Napoleon's Life in His Own Words* (London, 1911); F. M. Kircheisen: *Memoirs of Napoleon* (English edition); *Napoleon's Autobiography* (American edition, New York, 1931); Somerset de Chair: Napoleon Emperor of the French, *Memoirs,* (1950), changing the Caesarian third person to the first. J. Christopher Herold's *The Mind of Napoleon* was issued in 1955. Of these, *The Corsican* was the most successful. But the work still remains to be done in a critical spirit and with brief but adequate references.

IV. MEMOIRS BY CONTEMPORARIES

It is greatly to be lamented that the memoirs of the protagonists should be of such doubtful value: Talleyrand's are disappointing, Fouché's wholly unreliable. Practically all members of the imperial connection and most marshals wrote their memoirs or had them ghost-written at the time of the great Napoleonic vogue under Louis-Philippe. Few of them are of commanding value, with two exceptions, both edited by Major Jean Hanoteau: *The Memoirs of Queen Hortense* (2 vols., London, 1927), and *The Memoirs of Caulaincourt* (London, 1936).

The minor contemporaries come out rather better. I can specially recommend:

For Napoleon's early career: A. L. de Bourrienne.
For court gossip: Duchess of Abrantès (Laure Permon, Madame Junot); and Mme de Rémusat.
For the political and administrative world: A. C. Thibaudeau.
For army life: J. B. de Marbot. (There is a charming abridgement, with sprightly illustrations: *Adventures of General Marbot*, by John W. Thompson, Jr., New York, 1935.)
For the life of the common soldier: the fullest and most engaging: *Cahiers du Capitaine Coignet*, edited by Loredan Larchey (Paris, n.d.).

V. LITERATURE

The Napoleonic saga is pictorial rather than literary. It lives in monuments, statues, paintings, popular prints, and bric-à-brac rather than in epic poems, novels or dramas. As a guide (for French literature only) see my *Reflections on the Napoleonic Legend* (London and New York, 1924), part III. The results of many seminars on the Napoleonic legend in Western literature have not been published.

Among the headliners: F. R. de Chateaubriand: *Mémoires d'Outre-tombe* (1849-50). A whole book devoted to Napoleon, surprisingly fair, magnificent in style. Reprinted separately in Collection Nelson. The Battle of Waterloo in Victor Hugo's *Les Misérables* (1862); in sharp contrast with the account of the same battle, totally unrecognizable, in Stendhal's *La Chartreuse de Parme* (1839). (Stendhal never completed a long-projected *Life of Napoleon*.)

H. de Balzac: the first chapter in *La Femme de Trente Ans* (1831). *Le Napoléon du Peuple:* story of Napoleon told in a barn, in *Le Médecin de Campagne* (1833). *Une Ténébreuse Affaire* (1841). Alfred de Vigny: The Life and Death of Captain Renaud, in *Grandeur and Servitude of the Soldier* (1835). A fine study of *séidisme* or fanatical hero-worship; with the famous scene between Napoleon and Pius VII at Fontainebleau.

Leo Tolstoy: *War and Peace* (1865-9). The impact of Napoleon upon Russian society. The campaigns of 1805 and 1812. Long disquisitions against the "heroic individual" conception of history.

Thomas Hardy: *The Dynast* (1904-6): a great epic and philosophical drama of the Napoleonic age; with proper roles assigned to the Spirit Ironic and the Spirit of the Years.

Joseph Conrad left unfinished a novel, *Suspense:* the uneasy lull while Napoleon was in Elba; and in retrospect, the crushing dullness of society under the Empire (this chiefly from the *Memoirs* of Countess de Boigne).

INDEX

ABOUKIR, BAY OF (Battle of the Nile), 44–6
Acre, 22, 46
Ajaccio, 17, 20, 24, 26, 27
Alexander I, Czar of Russia, 71, 79, 85, 98, 112, 116, 123–4, 134, 136, 137–40, 141–2, 143, 144, 145, 146, 150, 167–8, 189
Alvinzi, 40
Amiens, Peace of, 59, 75, 79
Ancients, Council of, 52–3
Angell, Sir Norman, 103
Antommarchi, Francesco, 193–4, 197
Arndt, Ernst Moritz, 160
Arnott, Neil, 198
Aron, Robert, 184
Aspern, Battle of, 116, 130, 148
Aubigné, Agrippa d', 35
Aubry de la Boucharderie, Count Claude Charles, 29
Auerstädt, Battle of, 96–7, 183
Augereau, Pierre François Charles, 42, 50, 93, 94, 97, 163–4, 168
Austerlitz, Battle of, 91, 94, 95, 100, 104, 112, 114, 137, 148, 161, 179
Austria, 37, 38, 47, 58–9, 89, 91, 94–5, 114, 116, 117, 118, 123–5, 140, 156, 160, 161, 162, 173, 192
Autun, Bishop of, 51, 171
Autun, College of, 20–1

BABEUF, FRANÇOIS NOEL, 49
Bagration, Peter, Prince, 146, 147
Balzac, Honoré de, 67, 78, 200
Barclay de Tolly, Prince Michael, 146, 147
Baring, Francis, 102
Barras, Paul François, Vicomte de, 17, 18, 32, 33, 34, 35, 36–7, 50, 51, 57; Memoirs, 34
Basel, Treaty of, 107, 155

Bausset, Louis de, 122
Bautzen, Battle of, 161
Baylen, Battle of, 111–2, 113, 114, 121, 130, 131
Beauharnais, Alexandre, Vicomte de, 34
Beauharnais, Eugene de, 34, 41, 56, 83, 84, 122, 123, 152, 154, 156, 159, 163, 186
Beauharnais, Hortense de, 34, 36, 56, 83, 188
Beauharnais, Josephine de, see Josephine, Empress of the French
Beaulieu, Jean Pierre de, 39, 40
Beaumarchais, Pierre Augustin Caron de, 48
Beethoven, Ludwig van, 86
Belle Poule, La (ship), 201
Bellerophon (ship), 190
Bellilote, see Pauline Fourès
Béranger, Pierre Jean de, 200
Berezina River, 79, 145, 152
Berlin Decree, 100–1
Bernadotte, Charles, Prince of Pontecorvo, 30, 93, 94, 115, 117, 119, 141, 160, 162, 163, 170
Bernardin de Saint-Pierre, Jacques Henri, 35; Paul and Virginia, 35
Berry, Charles Ferdinand, Duke of, 177
Berthier, Pierre Alexandre, Prince of Neûchatel, 87, 123, 146, 154, 166
Bertrand, Henri Gratien, Comte, 166, 193
Bessières, Jean Baptiste, 131
Beyle, Marie Henri, see Stendhal
Bismarck-Schönhausen, Prince Otto Eduard Leopold von, 79, 134, 155
Black Cardinals, 125
Blücher, Gebhard Leberecht von, 163, 164, 165, 182, 183, 186
Bonaparte, Carlo, 19–20, 22–3, 26, 198

209

Bonaparte, Caroline, 23, 41, 53, 115, 122

Bonaparte, Eliza, Grand Duchess of Tuscany, 20, 23, 26, 41, 96, 129

Bonaparte, Jerome, King of Westphalia, 23, 83, 96, 122,123, 146,

Bonaparte, Joseph, King of Naples, 17, 20, 23, 24–5, 26, 30, 41, 83, 96, 104, 109, 110, 112, 115, 122, 130, 143, 188

Bonaparte, Léon, Comte, 122

Bonaparte, Letizia, 17, 19, 20, 27, 41, 64, 83, 84, 175, 193

Bonaparte, Louis, King of Holland, 23, 41, 83, 84, 96, 103, 110, 122, 128

Bonaparte, Lucciano, Archdeacon at Ajaccio, 20, 23

Bonaparte, Lucien, Prince of Canino, 20, 21, 23, 27, 52, 53, 76, 83, 109, 181, 185

Bonaparte, Napoleon, see Napoleon I, Emperor of the French

Bonaparte (Borghese), Pauline, 23, 41, 53, 175, 198

Borodino, Battle of, 145, 148, 161

Bossuet, Jacques Bénigne, 63

Boulay de la Meurthe, Antoine Jacques, Comte, 70

Brice, Raoul, 197; The Riddle of Napoleon, 197

Brienne, 21, 22, 23, 165

Brune, Guillaume Marie Anne, 47

Buonavita, Abbé, 194

Burke, Edmund, 75

CABARRUS, FRANÇOIS, 33

Cadoudal, Georges, 67–9, 72

Cambacérès, Jean Jacques Regis de, Duke of Parma, 53, 55, 60–1, 70, 84–5, 118, 128, 132

Cambronne, Pierre Jacques Etienne, Comte de, 184

Campoformio, Treaty of, 40, 42, 53, 118

Capet, Hugh, 71

Carlyle, Thomas, 32

Carnot, Lazare Nicholas Marguerite, 37–8, 40, 66, 82, 89, 142, 160, 180, 182, 185, 186, 187

Carteaux, Jean François, 28

Catherine ("the Great") Empress of Russia, 41, 136

Caulincourt, Armand Augustin Louis, Marquis de, 69, 70, 84, 123, 139, 141, 147, 154, 165, 166, 167, 180, 181

Champagny, Jean Baptiste Nompère, Comte de, 113, 127

Charlemagne, 86, 88, 105, 123, 125, 193

Charles, Archduke of Austria, 38, 40, 116

Charles III, King of Spain, 108, 113

Charles IV, King of Spain, 108, 136

Charles X, King of France, 199

Chasseloup-Laubat, Prosper de, 152

Chateaubriand, François René, Vicomte de, 62, 69, 171, 194, 199, 200; Génie du Christianisme, 62

Chatham, Earl of, see William Pitt, the Younger

Chernishev, Prince Alexander Ivanovitch, 140

Civil Code, 60, 61

Clarke, Henri Jacques Guillaume, 38

Clary family, 30

Clary, Désirée, 30

Clary, Julie, 30

Clausewitz, Karl von, 158

Cockburn, Sir George, 190

Code Napoléon, 61, 78

Coignet, 94; Notebooks, 94

Coigny, Aimée de, 171

Concordat, 60–1, 62–4, 86, 104, 111, 159

Constant, Benjamin, 179–80, 194

Corneille, Pierre, 22, 76, 78, 189, 194

Corsica, 17, 18–19, 24, 25, 26,29, 47, 71

Corvisart des Marets, Jean Nicolas, 132, 197

Courier, Paul Louis 86

DANTON, GEORGES JACQUES, 75

Daru, Pierre Antoine, Comte, 146

David, Jacques Louis, 88

Davout, Louis Nicolas, Prince of Eckmühl, 94, 97, 117, 146, 152, 154, 162, 180, 182, 185

Desaix de Vegoux, Louis Charles Antoine, 43, 58

Diderot, Denis, 62, 136

Dos de Mayo, 110, 112, 114

Dostoievski, Fedor Mikahilovitch, 69

Dubois, Antoine, 132
Duchesnois, Catherine Josephine, 85
Dugommier, Jacques François, 28
Dupont de l'Etang, Pierre Antoine, 111
Duroc, Géraud Christophe Michel, 77, 84, 88, 98, 123, 146, 166, 193

EBLE, JEAN BAPTISTE, 152
Egypt, 27, 35, 43–6, 50, 56, 168, 176
Elba, 168, 170, 175, 176, 186, 189, 192
Enghien, Louis de Bourbon-Condé, Duke of, 67, 68–9, 82, 107, 152, 168
England, 27, 37, 43, 45, 58, 68, 74–5, 89, 90, 95, 96, 100–3, 105–6, 107, 112, 117, 135–6, 139, 162, 171, 173, 198
Erfurt, Treaty of, 112, 113, 116, 124, 138, 142, 165
Essling, Battle of, 116
Eylau, Battle of, 97, 117, 148

FERDINAND VII, King of Spain, 108–10, 131, 136, 164
Fesch, Cardinal Joseph, 20, 87, 123, 125, 193, 194
Fichte, Johann Gottlieb, 158; Addresses to the German Nation, 158
Fisher, H. A. L., 184
Foch, Ferdinand, 76, 91
Fouché, Joseph, Duke of Otranto, 51, 59, 66, 70, 72–3, 82, 85, 87, 102, 110, 114–5, 119–20, 122, 123, 127, 128–9, 152, 180–1, 186, 187
Fourès, Pauline, 46
Fox, Charles James, 90, 100
Francis I, Emperor of Austria, 137
Francis I, King of France, 56
Frederick II ("the Great"), King of Prussia, 41, 79, 137, 158
Frederick William II, King of Prussia, 137, 158
Friedland, Battle of, 91, 97, 100, 113, 118, 137, 142, 148, 161

GABRIEL, JACQUES ANGE, 22
George III, King of England, 27, 57, 136

George IV, King of England, 136, 189, 192
Gneisenau, August Wilhelm Anton, Count Neithart von, 158, 183
Godoy, Manuel de, 89, 106, 107, 108, 109
Goethe, Johann Wolfgang von, 31, 85, 112, 156
Gohier, Louis Jerome, 50, 52
Gonnard, Philippe, 195; L'Oeuvre historique de Napoléon à Sainte-Hélène, 195
Gourgaud, Gaspard, Baron, 193, 194, 195
Goya y Lucientes, Francisco, 108; Caprichos, 108
Grouchy, Emmanuel, Marquis de, 183–4

HARDENBERG, PRINCE KARL AUGUST VON, 158
Henri IV, King of France, 93, 174, 175
Hitler, Adolph, 76
Hoche, Lazare, 34, 38, 42
Hofer, Andreas, 117
Hohenlinden, Battle of, 59, 68
Houssaye, Henri, 183
Hugo, Victor, 132, 196, 199, 200
Hulin, Pierre, 70, 152
Hundred Days, 55, 83, 175–90

Inconstant (ship), 176
Isabey, Jean Baptiste, 88
Italy, 35, 95, 146, 157, 159, 163, 165, 182

JACOBINS, 29, 33, 51, 52, 57, 67, 82, 119, 128, 129, 178, 195
Jefferson, Thomas, 101, 107
Jena, Battle of, 91, 96–7, 100, 112, 141, 158, 161, 183
Joffre, Joseph Jacques Césaire, 145
Joinville, François Ferdinand d'Orléans, Prince de, 201
Joseph II, Holy Roman Emperor, 18
Josephine, Empress of the French, 32, 34–6, 42, 46, 56–7, 68, 83, 84, 87–8, 98–9, 122, 125, 174, 187, 194, 198
Joubert, Barthélemy Catherine, 43, 50

Jourdan, Jean Baptiste, Comte, 38, 130
Junot, Andoche, Duke of Abrantes, 77, 106–7, 112

KANT, IMMANUEL, 80; Zweckmässigkeit ohne Zweck, 80
Kellermann, François Christophe de, Duke of Valmy, 38, 58, 133
Kléber, Jean Baptiste, 43, 46
Körner, Karl Theodor, 160
Krüdener, Barbara Juliana, Baroness von, 137
Kurakin (Russian Ambassador), 140, 141, 143
Kutusov, Michael Ilarionovitch Golenishtchev, 147–8, 150, 152, 158

LABEDOYERE, CHARLES DE, 177, 189
Laclos, Pierre Ambroise Choderlos de, 194
Lafayette, Marie Joseph du Motier, Marquis de, 48, 72, 170, 181, 186, 187
La Harpe, Frédéric César de, 137
Lamartine, Alphonse Marie Louis de, 199, 200
Lanjuinais, Jean Denis, 181
Lannes, Jean, Duke of Montebello, 77, 94, 114
Las Cases, Emmanuel Augustin, 193, 194; Mémorial de Sainte-Hélène, 194
Latouche-Tréville, Louis de, 89
Lebrun, Charles François, 53, 55, 70, 84, 128
Leclerc, Charles Victor Emmanuel, 53, 119
Lefebvre, Pierre François Joseph, Duke of Danzig, 52, 166
Legion of Honour, 60, 78
Leipzig, Battle of, 79, 163
Leopold II, Holy Roman Emperor, 18
Lessing, Gotthold Ephraim, 78
Longwood (house), 191, 198
Louis XIV, King of France, 56, 63, 85
Louis XV, King of France, 19
Louis XVI, King of France, 21, 41, 55, 128, 172, 179

Louis XVIII, King of France, 57, 171, 173, 174, 175, 178, 179, 187, 188
Louis-Philippe, King of France, 201
Louisiana, 61, 75, 107
Lowe, Sir Hudson, 192, 193, 197
Lunéville, Treaty of, 59, 118
Lützen, Battle of, 160

MABLY, GABRIEL BONNOT DE, 24
Macdonald, Alexandre, 117, 143, 158, 162, 166
Mackinder, Sir Halford, 139
Mack von Leiberich, Karl, Baron, 94
Madelin, Louis, 82, 93
Mahan, Alfred Thayer, 75
Maintenon, Françoise d'Aubigné, Marquise de, 23
Malet, Claude François de, 72, 152
Maleville, Jacques de, 60
Malmaison, La, 36, 57, 123, 188
Marbeuf, Comte de, 20
Marchand, General, 177
Marengo, Battle of, 58, 60, 68, 115, 152
Maret, Hugues Bernard, Duke of Bassano, 85, 157, 166
Maria Luisa, Queen of Spain, 106, 108
Maria Theresa, Empress of Austria, 41
Marie-Antoinette, Queen of France, 124, 125, 128
Marie-Louise, Empress of the French, 36, 124–7, 168, 175
Marmont, Auguste Frédéric Louis Viesse de, Duke of Ragusa, 93, 94, 117, 156, 166
Masséna, André, Prince of Essling, 43, 47, 94, 117, 130–2, 176
Melas, Michael, 58
Menou, Jacques François de, 31
Metternich - Winneburg, Clemens Wenzel Lothar, 77, 117, 124, 125, 161, 168, 173
Michelet, Jules, 200
Minims (religious order), 21
Miollis, Charles François, 105
Moncey, Bon Adrien Jeannot de, Duke of Conegliano, 166
Mont Saint Jean, see Waterloo
Montagnards, 67
Montesquieu, Charles de Secondat, Baron de La Brède et de, 24

Montholon, Charles Tristan, Comte de, 192–3, 197, 198
Moore, Sir John, 114, 130
Moreau, Jean Victor Marie, 38, 43, 50, 52, 59, 67, 68, 82, 115, 160
Mortier, Edouard Aldolphe Casimir Joseph, Duke of Treviso, 165, 182,
Morvan, J., 93; *Le Soldat Impérial*, 93
Moscow, 95, 145, 147, 148, 149–51, 152
Moulins, General, 50, 52
Muiron (frigate), 46
Murat, Joachim, King of Naples, 32, 53, 70, 84, 96, 109, 110, 115, 146, 147, 154, 160, 189

NAPOLEON I, Emperor of the French: birth, 17; education, 20–2; early military experience, 23–5; flight from Ajaccio, 27; capture of Toulon, 27–8; and Desirée Clary, 30; general for Thermidorians, 30–2; marriage to Josephine, 35–7; Italian campaign, 37–40; Egyptian campaign, 42–7; return from Egypt, 47; seizure of government, 50–3; First Consul, 53–7; second Italian campaign, 58; Civil Code, 60–1; Concordat, 61–4; Consul for Life, 65; attempted assassination and reprisals, 67–8; and Tallyrand, 70–2; character, 75–80; Emperor, 71; consecration by Pius VII, 86–7; coronation, 87–8; abortive attempt at invasion of England, 89–91; the beginning of the Continental War (Napoleonic War) 91; Austerlitz, 94–5; Jena and Auerstädt, 96–7; Friedland and the Peace of Tilsit, 97–8; the Berlin Decree, 100–3; conflict with Pope and excommunication, 104–5; the Portugal campaign, 105–7; the Spanish campaign, 107–12; the Treaty of Erfurt, 112–13; the Spanish campaign continued, 113–14; Paris plot against Napoleon, 114–16; Battle of Wagram, 117–18; divorce from Josephine, 122–3; marriage to Marie-Louise, 124–5; influence of Marie-Louise, 125–8; restoration of court in France and reaction, 127–8; birth of Napoleon II, 132;

Russian campaign, 134–54; causes and events leading to open war, 134–41; opening of the campaign, 146; Battle of Smolensk, 147; Battle of Borodino, 148–9; capture of Moscow, 149–50; retreat, 151–54; Battle of Lützen, 160–1; Battle of Leipzig (Battle of the Nations), 163; war in France, 164–6; abdication, 167–185; banishment to Elba, 168; escape from Elba and triumphal return, 175–9; Waterloo, 183–4; St. Helena, 190–8; writings about Napoleon and his own *Memoirs*, 194–7; illness, 197–8; his death, 198; burial at Hutsgate, 198; the Legend, 199–201; transfer of remains to Paris, 201
Napoleon II, (François Charles Joseph), 132–3, 181, 185–6, 195
Narbonne-Lara, Louis, Comte de, 142
National Guards, 27, 119
Neipperg, Adam Adelbert von, Count, 168
Nelson, Horatio, Viscount, 44, 90
Neuhof, Baron Theodor von, 18
Ney, Michel, Marshal of France, Duke of Elchingen, Prince of Moskowa, 93, 94, 131, 146, 153, 162, 166, 177, 178, 182–3, 189
Northumberland (ship), 190, 192, 193

O'MEARA, BARRY EDWARD, 193, 197
Ordener, Michel, 69
Organic Articles, 63, 87
Orient (ship), 44
Osterode, Castle of, 97
Oudinot, Nicolas Charles, 117, 151, 162, 166
Ouvrad, Gabriel Julien, 49, 51, 102

PALAFOX, JOSÉ DE, Duke of Saragossa, 114
Paoli, Pasquale, 18, 22, 25
Pasquier (Prefect of Police), 152
Patterson, Elizabeth, wife of Jerome Bonaparte, 83
Permon family, 106
Petit, Jean Martin, 168
Phélippeaux, Antoine de, 22, 46

Pilsudsky, Joseph, 138
Pisa, 18, 19, 25
Pitt, William, the Elder, Earl of Chatham, 90
Pitt, William, the Younger, 119
Pius VII, 62, 85, 86, 87, 104, 105, 168
Plaigne, Denuelle de la, 122
Pläswitz, Armistice of, 161
Plutarch, 22
Ponte Nuovo, 19
Portalis, Jean Etienne Marie, 60
Porto Ferraio, 176
Priestley, J. B., 75
Prudhomme, Joseph, 75
Prussia, 37, 50, 59, 91, 96–8, 126, 137, 138, 140–1, 156, 158, 160, 161, 162, 168

RACINE, JEAN BAPTISTE, 35; Athaliah, 35
Raynal, Guillaume Thomas François, 24
Reichstadt, Duke of, see Napoleon II
Robespierre, Augustin, 28
Robespierre, Maximilien, 28, 29, 30, 49, 52, 67, 72
Roger-Ducos, Pierre, 50, 53, 55
Rome, King of, see Napoleon II
Roosevelt, Franklin D., 76, 126
Rostopchin, Feodor Vasilyevitch, 145, 149
Rothschilds, 102
Rouget de Lisle, Claude Joseph, 86; Marseillaise, 86
Rousseau, Jean-Jacques, 19, 24, 62, 76, 77, 134
Rückert, Friedrich, 160
Russia, 45, 47, 59 89, 91, 95, 96, 97, 116, 124, 131, 133, 134–54 (the Russian campaign), 155, 158, 160, 161, 162, 192

SAINT-CYR, 23, 26
Saint-Germain, Charles Louis, Comte de, 21
St. Helena, 80, 121, 144, 175, 190, 191–201
Saliceti, Antoine Christophe, 38
Sans-Gêne, Mme (Mme Lefebvre), 52
Savary, Anne Jean Marie René, Duke of Rovigo, 70, 72, 127, 129, 152

Scharnhorst, Gerhard Johann David von, 158
Schenkendorf, Max von, 160
Schill, Ferdinand von, 117
Schönbrunn (palace), 94, 104, 117, 155
Schwarzenberg, Karl Philipp, 143, 151, 163, 164, 165
Scott, Sir Walter, 199
Sévigné, Marie de Rabutin-Chantal, Marquise de, 101
Siéyès, Emmanuel Joseph, 50, 53–5, 72, 166, 180; What is the Third Estate, 50
Smith, Sir William Sidney, 46
Smolensk, Battle of, 145, 147, 148, 150, 152
Sorel, Albert, 88
Soult, Nicholas-Jean de Dieu, 94, 114, 130, 131, 177, 178, 182
Spain, 37, 75, 77, 89, 105, 106, 107–12, 113, 116, 126, 130, 131, 133, 136, 141, 142, 157
Staël - Holstein, Anne Louise (Necker), Baroness of, 58, 76, 179
Stein, Heinrich Karl von zum, Baron, 144, 158, 160
Stendhal (Marie Henri Beyle), 86 194
Suchet, Louis Gabriel, Duke of Albufera, 163
Supper at Beaucaire, The (pamphlet by Napoleon), 27, 196
Suvorov, Alexander Vasilyevitch, 148

Talleyrand-Périgord, Charles Maurice de, 34, 41, 43, 45, 51, 57, 58, 59, 70–3, 85, 87, 88, 95, 98, 99, 107, 110, 113, 114–6, 123, 124, 127, 138, 157, 165, 170–3, 194, 199 Memoirs, 70
Tallien, Jean Lambert, 33, 34, 57
Tallien, Thérèse, 33, 34
Tarle, Eugene, 134; Napoleon's Invasion of Russia, 134
Teil, Général du, 28
Thiers, Louis Adolphe, 92, 200
Tilsit, Peace of, 98, 112, 116, 118, 137, 138, 142
Tolstoy, Leo Nikolayevitch, 148, 153
Toulon, 27, 28, 31, 43, 44, 106

Toussaint l'Ouverture, Pierre Dominique, 168
Trafalgar, Battle of, 90, 107, 121
Tronchet, François Denis, 60

UHLAND, JOHANN LUDWIG, 160
Ulm, Battle of, 90
Undaunted (ship), 168

VALENCE, 23, 24, 26
Valutina-Gora, Battle of, 145
Vandamme, Dominique René, 162
Vauban, Sébastian le Prestre de, 21
Victor Amadeus, King of Sardinia, 39
Victor, Claude Victor Perrin, called, 151, 152
Vienna, Congress of, 73, 173, 175
Vicnali, Abbé Ange, 194
Vigny, Alfred de, 159, 199, 200
Villeneuve, Pierre Charles, 89, 91
Vitrolles, Eugène, Baron de, 171
Voltaire (François Marie Arouet), 18, 62, 77–8; *Candide*, 18

WAGRAM, BATTLE OF, 91, 117, 119, 130, 155
Walewska, Marie, Countess, 98, 123, 175
Walewski, Alexander Colonna, Count, 98
Washington, George, 57, 79
Waterloo, Battle of, 80, 183–4, 186
Wellington, Arthut Wellesley, Duke of, 79, 112, 130–1, 136, 164, 182–4, 187
Wieland, Christophe Martin, 112
Wilson, Woodrow, 126, 173
Wittgenstein, Ludwig Adolf, 151, 152, 160
Wrede, Prince Karl Philipp, 163
Würmser, Dagobert Sigmund, Count von, 40

YORK AND ALBANY, Frederick Augustus, Duke of, 156, 158

ZOLA, EMILE, 17